Information Technology

Mergers, Acquisitions and Alternative Corporate Strategies
Hill Samuel Bank Limited

Tax: Strategic Corporate Tax Planning
Price Waterhouse

Finance for Growth
National Westminster Bank PLC

Company Law and Competition
S J Berwin & Co

Marketing: Communicating with the Consumer
D'Arcy Masius Benton & Bowles

Information Technology: The Catalyst for Change
PA Consulting Group

Marketing to the Public Sector and Industry
Rank Xerox Limited

Transport and Distribution
TNT Express

Property
Edward Erdman

Employment and Training
Blue Arrow PLC

Audio cassette documentaries are available on each of the titles above, showing through case studies, and interviews with senior executives, how British companies can take advantage of new markets in Europe. The cassettes are available at £12.95 through bookshops or from Didasko Ltd, Didasko House, Wennington, Huntingdon, Cambs PE17 2LX.

Information Technology:
The Catalyst for Change

PA Consulting Group

*With a Foreword by
the Hon. Douglas Hogg, MP
Minister for Industry and Enterprise*

Published in association with
CBI Initiative 1992

MERCURY BOOKS
Published by W.H. Allen & Co. Plc

First published in 1990
by the Mercury Books Division of
W.H. Allen & Co. Plc
Sekforde House, 175–9 St John Street, London EC1V 4LL

Set in Plantin by Phoenix Photosetting, Chatham
Printed and bound in Great Britain by
Butler & Tanner Ltd, Frome, Somerset

British Library Cataloguing in Publication Data

Information technology
   1. Business firms. Computer systems
   I. PA Consulting Group
   II. CBI Initiative 1992
   658'.05

ISBN 1–85251–042–0

Contents

Foreword

I am pleased that the CBI decided to include information technology as one of the business themes of their Initiative 1992. We are all aware of the major impact IT has on the efficiency and competitiveness of firms operating throughout the economy. I believe that IT will be a crucial element as UK firms prepare for the challenge of the single market in Europe.

But what does the single European market mean for the IT marketplace? The IT industry has been used to operating against the background of European and international competition, and for some time now it has not been possible to think purely in terms of national markets in the IT field. New technology has had the effect of driving away many of the barriers to trade. But some still remain and it is these that member states of the Community are now taking action to remove. This is especially so in relation to IT standards.

IT has brought untold benefits by enabling firms and people to do things differently and by creating whole new products and new types of services. But realising the full potential of these benefits usually depends on the existence of agreed standards: standards to allow for the interconnection and interworking of equipment; standards to foster the creation of European or international markets rather than national ones; or standards to make the technology easier for customers to handle.

Users of IT are well used to coping with the rapid and continuous changes in the technology itself. IT users are also now beginning to take advantage of the greater flexibility and freedom that open systems standards provide. But a crucial challenge facing those responsible for providing efficient and effective information systems stems from the creation of the single market itself. It is widely acknowledged that firms with the best and most effective information systems are those that have a clear and well thought out information systems strategy: a strategy which forms an integral part of their overall business strategy.

Those responsible for information systems need to be fully aware of the way their firm intends to tackle the challenge of the single market. But the planning and installation of new information systems cannot be achieved overnight. The best systems will be those that have been carefully planned and executed.

The UK is in the lead in pressing for an open and competitive single market, and the Government is deeply committed to achieving it. We are not the reluctant Europeans you read about. We play a leading role and we are winning the argument for a deregulated enterprising Europe.

But it is vitally important for firms at home to be aware of the changes; to be aware of the single market challenge. For there is no doubt that all businesses will be affected. Many measures have already been agreed and will be implemented well before the end of 1992. Action to prepare cannot be left until the last minute: by then it will be too late.

A crucial element in the plans of successful firms will undoubtedly be their information systems: systems that provide management with the information that it needs; systems that can help firms to tackle the challenges of the single market; systems that provide accurate and timely data; systems that are up and running as a firm adjusts its business strategy to take advantage of the opportunities arising in the single market.

All this adds up to a single clear message. Firms must act now to prepare adequately for the single market, and a crucial element in those plans will be the development of their information systems.

I congratulate PA Consulting Group and the CBI on their efforts to help businesses prepare for the challenges ahead.

The Hon. Douglas Hogg, MP
Minister for Industry and Enterprise

Preface

The underlying premise of this book is that the single market is a rare opportunity, unlikely to be repeated in the lives of most senior corporate management, and that one important way to prepare an organisation for the wholesale changes that will be needed to survive in a post-1992 environment is embodied in the theory and application of information technology.

It also examines how the culmination of forty years of technological innovation is about to bear fruit and alter radically the way we perceive what constitutes business activity, how we formulate our business tactics and strategies, how we view our competitors, and ultimately how companies will need to evolve rapidly to survive one of the most concentrated periods of change ever recorded.

This book shows how to cope with two inevitable upheavals and how to combine them into one manageable event. It will explain how information technology (IT) will facilitate preparations for 1992 and how the single market will allow companies to derive the maximum benefit from IT.

The initial four chapters deal with the opportunities presented to everyone in Europe by the 1992 timetable. Whereas the UK has been historically reluctant to throw in its lot with the rest of Europe, we possess some of the necessary pre-requisites for success but we certainly do not hold a monopoly on virtue.

By breaking down barriers between markets in the run-up to 1992 and by dismantling inefficiencies within organisations through a creative use of IT, a totally new force will be created: the single information market. The characteristics of this single market in information have already been largely determined by the technological undercurrents that have flowed through organisations in the past fifteen years. A few important uncertainties remain, such as whether Europe, or even the UK, has a role to play in the IT world of the future and whether the attempt to create common IT standards will be a help or a hindrance to progress.

Faced with the impending upheavals triggered by 1992 and the rapid evolution of IT, organisations will be forced to rely more than ever on a coherent business strategy. This will need to be flexible enough to be adapted to rapidly changing circumstances (or unforeseen opportunities) and sound enough to weather the near chaos that lies ahead as thousands of like-minded competitors fight for survival.

Part II looks at the way successful companies will need to develop an ethos of quality, regardless of pressures on product life-cycles or competitor innovation. These chapters also investigate the rise of the Euro-product and the type of fundamental changes which are expected to take place in the factories and the offices of the future. The role of IT in bringing about these large-scale changes is examined in detail.

The final five chapters of the book are concerned with the problems of successfully implementing a coherent IT strategy for 1992. Non-technical components of success are studied: executive vision and leadership; corporate culture and human resources; and the physical environment in which the company operates. Problems with managing continental-scale projects are scrutinised and the development of pan-European organisations is charted. The importance of effective management direction is stressed and an approach to managing major multi-country IT projects is recommended. This requires facing up to the opportunities, problems and conflicts at the start of the project, before significant financial investment is made. Proper planning and ongoing management will ensure that the benefits are realised.

A summary is provided of what primary and secondary actions are needed for a UK company to thrive in the EC after 1992 and of how an innovative use of IT will act as a catalyst for this change and enable the creation of sustained competitive advantage in the single market.

A range of case studies of successful IT projects concludes this section and features companies in the chemicals industry, the legal profession, newspaper publishing, car manufacture, food retailing, glass-making and aerospace engineering.

There are many people involved in a book of this kind but a particular mention must be made of Dr Gordon Ross, author, and Paul Hannon, who provided additional research material.

This is an important book for all sectors of UK commerce and industry. I commend it to you.

John Foden
Chief Executive, PA Consulting Group

I
The 1992 opportunity

1.　Winning in Europe

The opportunity

The EC presented UK industry with one of its greatest challenges in decades when it agreed to take the necessary steps towards building a single market. The industrial and political challenges are unique. They will never happen again.

By the time the single market becomes a reality, Europe will have enjoyed almost half a century of peace and rising prosperity. Europe is now attempting to rebuild itself on a scale similar to that undertaken after the Second World War and is hoping thereby to achieve the industrial economies of scale that have been denied it because of the historically fragmented nature of the market. The aim is to transform a patchwork of incompatible economies into a tapestry of open and unfettered competition. In doing so, domestic industries in different member states will be able to compete against each other as never before. In theory, a new unified market of 323 million consumers will be created. This will be the world's largest single market, even exceeding the markets of the USA and Japan.

New ground rules have been drawn up and, more significantly, new concepts of business are being forced on everyone across the Community. If a company is to survive it will need to think about operating in an EC-wide market. It must determine how its products will compete against those of West German or Italian companies and how it should differentiate its products both from Continental competition and from threats from outside the Community (notably from the USA and Japan). It must also find ways of achieving a full European presence, whether this is through growth or acquisition.

The transformation that has already taken place is evident in the sales and profits league tables for Europe. Apart from British Petroleum and the two Anglo-Dutch groups, Royal Dutch Shell and Unilever, the UK is not listed in the top twenty companies by turnover (Figure 1). German and French groups instead take the lion's share of Europe's industrial turnover. When we look, however, at a similar league table for profitability (Figure 2), we see the top six positions held by UK companies, followed by one only from Italy, the USA,

The new competition

Figure 1. Top twenty companies by turnover in Europe

	Company	Country	Turnover 1987 (million ecu)
1	Shell Group	Netherlands/UK	68,168
2	British Petroleum	UK	39,579
3	Daimler Benz	W Germany	32,713
4	Bundespost	W Germany	26,713
5	Volkswagen	W Germany	26,488
6	Fiat	Italy	25,221
7	Siemens	W Germany	24,934
8	Unilever	Netherlands/UK	23,755
9	Ford	USA	23,000
10	Philips	Netherlands	22,722
11	Nestlé	Switzerland	21,138
12	Renault	France	21,106
13	ENI	Italy	20,821
14	EXXON	USA	20,000
15	VEBA	W Germany	19,623
16	BASF	W Germany	19,508
17	EDF	France	19,421
18	CGE	France	18,237
19	Elf-Aquitaine	France	18,222
20	Bayer	W Germany	18,007

Figure 2. Top ten companies by profit in Europe

	Company	Country	Profit 1987 (billion ecu)
1	Shell Group	Netherlands/UK	4.1
2	British Petroleum	UK	3.4
3	British Telecom	UK	3.3
4	BAT Industries	UK	2.0
5	ICI	UK	1.9
6	British Gas	UK	1.8
7	Fiat	Italy	1.7
8	IBM	USA	1.6
9	Dir. Gen. Des Télécom.	France	1.3
10	Bundespost	W Germany	1.3

France and West Germany. When stock market capitalisation figures are taken into account, the strength and the potential of the UK industrial and financial sectors become obvious.

With a decade of wholesale industrial restructuring behind it, the UK finds itself in a relatively strong position to meet the challenge and seize the opportunities that the political initiative has spawned. Imagine how Europe as a whole would have coped if the single market timetable had been 1972. A devastating oil price shock was just around the corner, followed by years of rampant inflation and political uncertainty. The long-term goals of political and economic unity in Europe could have been damaged permanently.

Imagine how UK industry would have fared had the single market timetable been set for 1982 instead of 1992. The industrial confrontation with our European competitors would have been on less than equal terms. Ten years later, however, a leaner, fitter and more optimistic industry can look its Continental rivals squarely in the eye and know that it can compete.

UK handicapped by historic factors

UK's handicaps

The UK, however, suffers from two serious handicaps in competing with European industry. In addition to being on the periphery geographically of the Community, a small but historically significant stretch of water physically and psychologically separates the island from the mainland. Research on the regional impact of the single market has suggested that there is no guarantee that the prosperity stemming from 1992 will be uniformly distributed throughout the EC. In fact a key part of the Commission's strategy is to allocate resources to 'areas of greatest economic advantage'. These will be the regions closest to the EC's core – south-east England, southern Germany, northern France, northern Italy, and most of the Benelux countries, while geographically remote areas, regions with under-developed economies and areas with old and non-competitive industries will lose out.

Information technology (IT), however, can play a decisive role in diffusing the benefits of the single market throughout the Community. Local governments and businesses in some of the less favoured regions can fight back by:

● Improving production, sales and administration performance through the use of up-to-date IT

● Ensuring that the best IT infrastructures are in place both to attract new businesses and to support existing organisations in the efforts to compete

Geography has also reinforced the UK's second handicap – culture. The UK lacks the enthusiastic commitment to a unified market that France and West Germany display. The UK has also failed to show the same degree of support for a pan-European political and economic structure that our EC competitors see as the next stage in creating a cohesive Community. For them, 1992 is not an end in itself but part of a broader transition to a wholly new socio-economic order. Their business people are working hard to achieve that end.

UK companies' continuing references to doing business with 'Europe' illustrates the depth of the cultural problems that face us. By any definition of geography, the UK is part of Europe, yet we choose to look on ourselves as separate.

Opportunities from the single market

Since the natural boundaries of many businesses are determined by distribution economics, the removal of barriers will allow them to extend their catchment areas. Some estimates suggest that there will be a 20 to 30 per cent decline in lorry costs in the EC after the barriers come down, while rail transport, for which there are strong economic arguments beyond a 250-kilometre range, will also expand the marketability of products.

The Golden Circle

As an alternative to creating Euro-brands, there will be greater opportunities for selling existing products to different social groupings. Advertising agency D'Arcy Masius Benton & Bowles has constructed a map of EC consumers and identified the 'Golden Circle' – the region which contains the 50 million wealthiest Europeans. It does not conform to the traditional political and physical boundaries that exist in Europe but illustrates the groupings of people who make similar choices of products, and have similar social aspirations and lifestyles. Such an instrument of market research was not needed ten years ago – the commercial logic of such demography is now evident. It can be used to explain, and exploit, consumer patterns in the Community.

While market research will continue to be an important aid, it will be the creative ability to define new ways of looking at markets and consumers which will characterise the outstanding successes in the single market. Companies have to encourage their marketing entrepreneurs to improve their chances of success.

Vulnerability

Some markets will be vulnerable to the pressures of increased competition in Europe after 1992. There will be many companies in highly competitive sectors that will not withstand the onslaught of the new trading regime. The most vulnerable companies/markets will:

- Have a low value-added element

- Be exposed to low priced overseas producers

- Be unresponsive and uncompetitive

- Suffer from over-production and little product differentiation

Market niches

There can be minuscule market niches in tired, worn-out industries and there can be profit in being the last 'ice man' (now virtually defunct, the ice man delivered blocks of ice to households in the USA to preserve foodstuffs). The company that specialises in French polishing or repairing 1950s transistor radios may still have a future.

On a much larger scale, however, there have been suggestions that the EC is facing a north–south divide of its own and that the relatively heavily industrialised northern member states will prosper at the expense of the poorer, agriculturally based southern members that have recently joined the Community. After decades of paying for agricultural surpluses and embarrassing over-production, there are few in the EC that are calling for another round of expansion of the Community's food base. Instead the view is that the time has come for industry and commerce to benefit from a pan-European philosophy and that this will not cost the EC taxpayer anything like as much as the Common Agricultural Policy. The onus will be on the southern and peripheral regions to make the most of the new unfettered competition rather than relying on an inefficient food production economy.

Competition from outside EC

If some markets and regions are more vulnerable than others to the impact of the single market, a less obvious concern is the possibility of pre-emptive strikes by non-EC companies. The risk of being smothered by US, Japanese, Korean, Australian, or South African companies as they try to increase their toe-holds in Europe ahead of the free market is of growing concern. These companies know they may find it more difficult to establish bases in the EC after 1992 and are, therefore, prepared to buy key stakes in key industries. The most vulnerable will be high value-added consumer goods industries that are not manufacturing in their domestic markets, and leisure-related goods and service industries. This can span anything from food and drink to airlines and hotels, with much in between. Some foreign companies will also use 'Panamanian flagging' which operates in the world shipping industry and enables a company to gain a presence in a lax legislative environment so that it can trade in the more tightly regulated economies and benefit from low start-up costs and minimum infrastructure needs.

Mergers and acquisitions on the increase

In USA

When one looks at the level of UK merger and acquisition activity, the USA has been the natural home for UK funds and corporate hopes. In 1987, some 415 cross-border bids were made by UK companies and about two-thirds of these, representing about 95 per cent of the total value, were in the USA. The British have not been reluctant to make investments in North America over the past few decades but this has been very much on an *ad hoc* basis with some companies spotting cheap, undervalued targets that lend themselves to dedicated asset stripping. The type of investment that is required in the EC is more systematic and strategic and must be operated on clear focused lines. Only then will the requisite levels of profitability be achieved.

EC mergers will increase

Over the last five years there has been a large increase in the level of merger and acquisition activity within Europe. In 1987, there was a 45 per cent jump to 3,400 in the number of acquisitions in France, West Germany and the UK. Yet most of these were domestic and the proportion of cross-border bids has remained static since the mid-1980s. Most forecasts, however, predict a huge increase in cross-border merger activity in the next three years as organisations try to position themselves for the impact of the single market. This will have important implications for the IT strategy of an organisation because it will have to deal with the consequences of such mergers and acquisitions and establish order and interworking between incompatible computer systems.

What is needed is vision

Winning in the EC is more than simply surviving in the EC – although, for many, survival will be the first crucial goal. Whereas half a dozen major companies in any one industry in any country would have been the norm pre-1992, the expected shake-out is likely to deplete the ranks considerably, leaving perhaps just half a dozen key players in that industry within the entire EC. Small and medium-sized companies are forecast to be the most affected by a barrier-free European market. For them to win will require a re-examination of goals throughout their business.

Re-examine existing practices

Being forced to re-examine existing practices from top to bottom can provide some extraordinary benefits. In the mid-1970s, Toyota manufacturing engineers set out to match the existing world best time for the resetting of a body panel press (which was four hours). At that time Toyota was taking two days. They scrutinised the methods employed by other manufacturers and managed to achieve their four-hour goals at the Toyota plants. Shortly afterwards, senior management demanded that the resetting time be reduced to twelve minutes and this was subsequently achieved. The Toyota business strategy has changed so that the company now builds a car only after it has been sold. This fundamental change in approach challenged basic company-wide assumptions and produced a quantum leap in productivity.

A similar exercise at a European electronics plant required assembly lead time to be cut from one week to twenty-four hours, costs to be reduced by 20 per cent, quality to be improved to one part per million and twenty-four-hour delivery reliability to be improved to 95 per cent. The manufacturing engineers who were faced with this litany of demands on one product were amazed to discover not only that they were possible but that they could be achieved within existing resources. Setting 'impossible' targets can focus attention and resources, and sometimes such targets can even be met.

Going for gold

Organisations will find themselves at a crossroads where they will confront a bewildering choice of destinations. Depending on what form of transport and type of luggage they wish to use, they will head for corporate expansion, revolution, consolidation or breakthrough. Their decision will be determined by the level of resources that are allocated to the journey and the degree of change the company wishes to make.

Existing market leaders in any sector stand a good chance of competing with the best in the Community. Second-line companies that are prepared to do some serious soul-searching may have to conclude that their current business strategy, corporate productivity or research and development (R&D) are inadequate and need changing. Any necessary changes must be accomplished soon.

Companies looking to triumph will require excessive dedication – an obsession with winning which has been lacking in UK companies compared with our mainland European counterparts. Our low standing in terms of gross national product (GNP) and disposable wealth is testimony to past inabilities to grasp the nettle of modern business life.

Globalisation

One of the basic characteristics of modern business is the increasing international nature of commerce. The globalisation of markets is already well advanced with many examples in finance, energy, commodities, pulp and paper, electronics, cars and luxury goods. But markets will retain important local qualities. As competition in the EC increases, more niche markets will be served because the industrial technology will allow greater flexibility of product design, handling and distribution. European industry can then use its experience of serving diverse local markets to expand into global markets and benefit from the huge economies of scale that will follow.

A Community vision

In order to become world-class players from a European base, companies need to build a Community vision, a set of values and method of operating that will permeate all their activities. The corporate drivers for change (Figure 3) which embrace strategy, marketing, products, manufacturing, distribution, R&D, culture, finance and IT will be moulded by this Community approach. Whereas some mainland EC companies already take this stance for granted, this will be a considerable hurdle for many UK organisations needing to make up for decades of isolationism, protectionism and a tendency to look across the Atlantic rather than across the Channel.

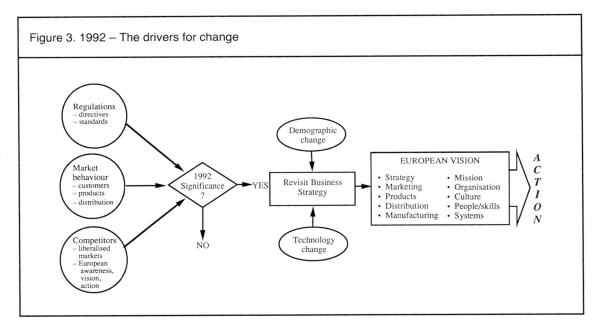

Figure 3. 1992 – The drivers for change

Quality a vital goal

Paramount in this redefinition of corporate vision will be the consumer. The traditional customer–business relationship will change mostly in the growing importance of consumer satisfaction. To satisfy growing customer demands, both UK and mainland European companies must take their lessons from abroad.

Total quality management

The concept of total quality management (TQM) is vital as a basis for expansion. TQM is an approach to business improvement led by quality, which embraces the entire company on the premise that every aspect of a company's operation ultimately affects the customer. This concept originated in the USA but did not find corporate backing there so the 'father' of quality, Dr W. Edwards Deming, took his ideas to Japan, where they were welcomed. Post-war Japan used the notion of total quality in an attempt to rebuild its shattered economy. It has proved to be one of the key ingredients of Japan's successful penetration of Western markets.

It took perhaps thirty years for US companies to accept the philosophy of 'total quality' and a further five to ten years before European industry realised what gains could be achieved. John A. Young, president and CEO of Hewlett-Packard, sums up his company's view of TQM: 'In today's competitive environment, ignoring the quality issue is tantamount to corporate suicide.' Few companies have shown more dedication to the pursuit of quality than Hewlett-Packard.

The UK's experience may not be so encouraging. 'British business is changing significantly in customer orientation and efficiency drives,' says Ian Nicol, a Pilkington Glass manager with particular experience of TQM. 'However, total quality management and all its jargon is seen by many as another "flavour of the month" and not a long-term business philosophy. The sceptics will not be convinced solely by pages of literature and numerous seminars. Those companies already benefiting from TQM must open their doors and share their experiences for the good of British business in total.' At the moment top European management does not take a very visible lead in quality management and even fewer monitor their quality against competitors'. If UK and other European companies are to compete in world markets, total quality management must be one of their strategies.

The cycle of quality (Figure 4) that exists in successful companies begins with focused management action which guarantees that quality work is carried out throughout the organisation. Competitive prices flow from this quality approach. This in turn generates perceptions of value in the market place. As more satisfied customers buy from the quality organisation, it increases its market share, which reinforces the total quality approach of management and encourages it to strive for even higher quality achievements. TQM will prove to be one guiding light for an industrial renaissance in Europe.

Figure 4. The quality cycle

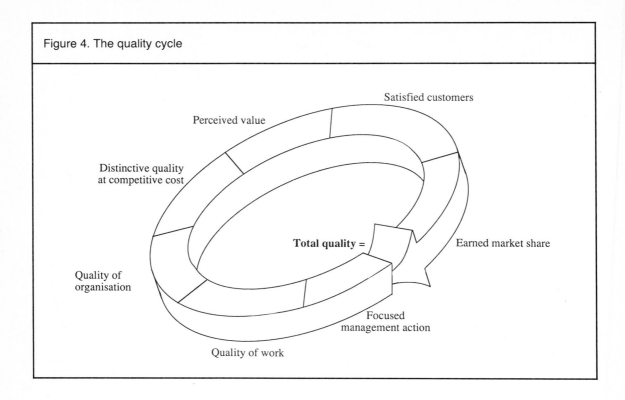

Satisfied customers

Perceived value

Distinctive quality
at competitive cost

Quality of
organisation

Total quality =

Earned market share

Focused
management action

Quality of work

Teamwork also vital

Companies will also need to look closely at how their organisations
actually work and how effective teamwork can be achieved at every
level in the company – from the doorman to the boardroom, from the
systems department to the shop floor. It can be summed up in the
word 'cohesion'. Companies that have a clear and limited set of shared
values driving their performance will be most likely to succeed in the
single market.

Employees will have to perform as members of the company first
and as office or factory workers second. There will be a growing need
to dismantle the barriers within organisations, to reduce demarcation
lines and to extract the maximum effort that employees can make. In
return employees can achieve higher levels of skill, greater job satisfaction, high job security and higher financial reward.

Just as the psychological and economic barriers are being pulled
down within the EC, so at company level a similar exercise will need to
take place. There will be a growing urgency for breeching the traditional corporate infrastructure and allowing a more 'open plan'

**Dismantle barriers
within organisations**

mentality to develop. There will be no room for Chinese walls. Cross-fertilisation of departments and teams will be crucial if a company is to meet the simultaneous demands of new markets in a large number of countries. Communication is therefore another key component for success.

Productivity still a problem

UK's productivity gap

The UK economy is based on relatively low earnings and low productivity. Recent strides in output have attempted to invert this formula so that industry can generate high earnings through higher productivity on the strength of more competitive unit costs and quality improvements. Despite the gains of recent years, the UK remains well down the league table of wealth creation. It is conceivable that the productivity gap between the UK and her European competitors may be narrowed or even bridged within the next decade, provided UK management accepts that radical reform of methods and practices is necessary. Lord Young tried to quantify the scale of the task in 1988 during a parliamentary debate on manufacturing productivity: 'There are arguments about the size of the gap, but I suspect we might be as much as 30 per cent behind some of our major competitors.'

Data produced by the CBI and PA suggest that if the UK could sustain growth of about 5 to 6 per cent per annum, it would take seven years to catch up with West German productivity levels and a total of eight years to equal French productivity. It could take over twenty years to bridge the gap with Japan, whereas US productivity is so advanced that the UK may never be able to equal it. We have to set higher targets and achieve them!

Need for capital investment

OECD data indicate that the UK showed some of the greatest gains in output per employee in manufacturing during the 1983–7 period. It posted an annual average increase of 5.8 per cent compared with Italy (5.6 per cent), the USA (5.5 per cent), Japan (5.0 per cent), France (2.8 per cent) and West Germany (2.6 per cent). The CBI has established a clear relationship between investment and productivity performance. In its crudest terms, the UK has experienced a productivity gap because there has been a prolonged investment gap. It becomes evident at this stage that our 'accounting mentality' is not serving us well in world markets. Current investment, however, has picked up, strongly suggesting that recent productivity growth will be of a more sustainable kind. The advent of the single market will intensify the need for even greater capital investment in many parts of industry.

The sophistication of today's market means that products no longer sell simply because they are cheap. It is, therefore, unrealistic to aim to be the lowest cost producer when product differentiation can be achieved through superior exploitation of quality, technology, time, customer service, or any combination of these factors. Price, however, is still important and companies must continually search for ways of improving value for money. Too many companies still associate the term 'increased productivity' with the labour resource of manufacture and fail to study other, often more critical, factors such as materials, energy, plant, capital, technology and time.

UK industry is now faced with the opportunity of a market of 323 million people. But it also faces eleven hardened industrial nations that have the same idea about carving up a very profitable portion of the EC's market potential. Several of those nations have done considerably better than us in the recent past and as a result are better prepared. The UK has to find new and innovative ways in which to compete.

The successful UK company in Europe after 1992 will be characterised by its quality of management. It will have displayed:

- Clarity of objectives and goals
- Willingness and ability to measure performance
- Close contact with the entire company
- Sensitivity and awareness to needs and opportunities
- Willingness to manage by walking about
- Success in establishing beach-heads in new markets

Flexibility and responsiveness

To survive in a highly competitive environment, a business must be able to respond quickly. This responsiveness to fluctuating market conditions will dictate the way a company is structured, the type of management it uses, production techniques, marketing, and its attitudes towards IT.

Need for faster innovation

The speed at which companies gear up to new market conditions and maintain a responsive posture will play a major role in determining their successes or failures in the single market. The speed at which markets are changing is also affecting the rate at which companies must innovate and change. A productivity gain that would have given a company five years of competitive advantage in 1980 will today only secure advantage for several months.

Greater pressure will be placed on the innovatory processes within the organisation. The marketing, mission and resource influences which shape ideas will be tested to the limit. The timescales for evaluating the options will be less generous than in the past. When the preferred route has been selected, the company must be prepared to go with the idea 100 per cent. Implementation will be carried out with surgical accuracy and the rewards will come to those brave enough to subject themselves to even more demanding criteria for the next innovation. The business enterprise of the future will be radically different from many that exist today.

Regional preferences will remain

Products will change as demand patterns shift. The Euro-product, which conjures up a spectre of bland, dehumanised consumer goods, is unlikely to make an appearance for a long time. Each market will continue to have its own particular requisites, peculiarities and preferences. Therein lies the difficulty and the attraction. 'England, Wales and Scotland have had a single market for hundreds of years, yet consumption patterns still vary widely by region,' says Clive Holland, Deputy Chairman of advertising group Young & Rubicam. 'Why is it that the Scots eat twice as much Fry's Chocolate Cream and drink twice the amount of Coca-Cola as the English?' he asks. Regional Spanish drinking habits also seem to defy understanding: beer in Catalonia, wine in Castile, whisky in Galicia and sherry in Andalucia. 'Despite the availability of most car types across Europe,' he continues, 'most of the car-buying population generally sticks to major national brands – Rover in Britain, Peugeot and Renault in France and Volkswagen in Germany.'

It will take time to break down these barriers and only by meeting consumer needs directly in a quality and value-for-money fashion will there be any chance of success.

Information technology and 1992

What role does IT play in 1992? IT, when it is well implemented, can be used to improve significantly the factors of quality, teamwork, communication and responsiveness. This book is about the opportunities IT offers and what must be done to achieve effective implementation.

IT can be used to interpret business trends and allows companies to offer customers the products they want. It can be a catalyst for change in an organisation – something that we in the UK find particularly difficult to achieve. The opportunity that 1992 represents for UK industry can be fully exploited only through a well-managed business strategy and within that the IT strategy will be a vital component. IT can give a company sustainable competitive advantage.

The impact of 1992 on the elements of a corporate business plan will mean a greater reliance on information technology reaching all the dimensions of the strategy. IT will run parallel with the company's efforts to serve its customers and expand its position in the market place. So prominent will the role of IT be in achieving this 1992 strategy, that some may be forgiven for assuming that the technology was the plan itself. IT will only yield sustainable competitive advantage if it is used solely to reach the targeted, focused business objectives.

The following chapters will illustrate how and why executives and managers must prepare now for the challenges of the single market after 1992.

Information technology: In the broadest sense IT is about computers and communications. More specifically IT deals with systems that capture, transmit, process, store and retrieve information. With proper management, it can magnify the talent and skills of a company's staff and open up new areas of business. If not properly controlled, it can mis-direct corporate energy, waste valuable resources and damage a company's competitiveness.

---

2. The single information market

The information resource

In the early 1980s, management theorists began to examine the role of information as a resource within companies and to move away from the position that computers and information processing were simply service activities that aided rather than directed a company's activities. Prior to this a computer budget was in the same category as office utilities – something that a company needed but which always remained in the background, allowing the firm to get on with its real business. Now information has become recognised as the lifeblood of an organisation (Figure 5). Without information, the modern organisation is dead.

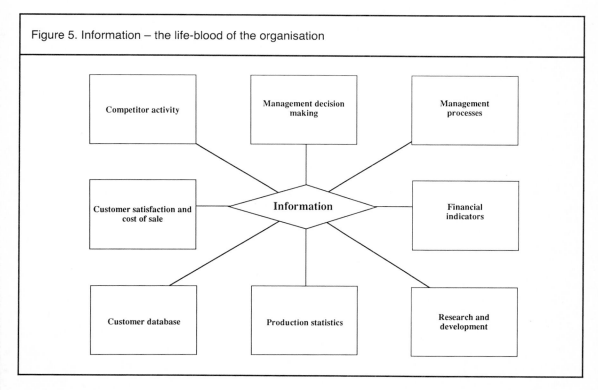

Figure 5. Information – the life-blood of the organisation

Competitor activity

Management decision making

Management processes

Customer satisfaction and cost of sale

Information

Financial indicators

Customer database

Production statistics

Research and development

The position changed as academic research started to break new ground. One of the key thinkers who encouraged businesses to take a fresh look at the constituents of commercial success was Michael Porter, a Harvard Business School lecturer and business consultant. From 1980, Porter's seminal *Competitive Strategy* (Collier Macmillan, 1985) became required reading for top management because it defined important characteristics of modern business competition in the form of a number of primary 'forces'. He also outlined three generic strategies for achieving competitive advantage: cost leadership, differentiation and focus.

These strategies were advanced in his next book *Competitive Advantage – Creating and Sustaining Superior Performance* (Collier Macmillan, 1985). This showed management how to go about implementing the strategies of the first book. The most important factor in achieving a competitive advantage was an understanding of how a company actually worked. His diagnostic tool was the 'value chain', which could identify opportunities for competitive advantage to be generated. Helped by contributions from other academics, information and IT were elevated to a more serious position in the ranks of management analysis. Some companies began to claim that information and the technology that enveloped it were strategic resources and offered the potential of competitive advantage.

IT as a strategic weapon

Figure 6 illustrates how IT can develop into a competitive weapon.

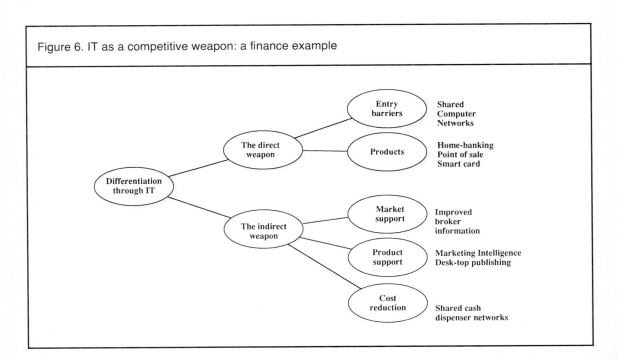

Figure 6. IT as a competitive weapon: a finance example

IT can provide product differentiation, both directly and indirectly, which can lead to the creation of entry barriers, new products, market support, product support and cost reductions. Unfortunately many companies still regard such technology as a support tool, not as a strategic weapon.

Information and IT

Information and IT are interdependent. A system must be installed before any strategic advantage can be gained and the data must be available for the system to use. Information does not follow the rules that apply to other resources. It can be used more than once, often with different effects. The value that it generates for the company often depends on 'outside' factors such as the manager that is handling the information, the state of the company's business position or the overall market. Its inherent value can be increased by a reduction in the amount of raw data and an increase in the information made available through filtering or additional analysis. A Yellow Pages business telephone directory is a sample of raw data that is transformed into valuable information by the actions of a telephone caller. This directory will be used dozens or hundreds of times for different reasons and each telephone call can have a different value to the person or company.

The application of information has a number of qualities. It can be used to gain a competitive edge over rivals, but its effectiveness will be blunted over time. Any item of information will have a limited lifespan or 'shelf-life'. It may be vital one week and of little value the next. A one-off competitive gain does not produce lasting strategic advantage. What should be sought is sustained competitive advantage flowing from a strategic decision made by a company.

IT is one of the essential building blocks of the modern organisation. It is linked to R&D, finance and administration, manufacturing and logistics, and sales and marketing. Its impact is felt in many aspects of the company's activities and will alter the nature of human resources, project management, work simplification and organisational change. IT should not be the foundation of the company – an organisation's business strategy should be that – but it should serve as a tool to implement this strategy and as a glue to hold the diverse activities together.

IT implements business strategy

There is an important distinction between information and IT. They could both be described as information resources but the terms should not be used interchangeably. IT is easily defined in terms of computing power, number of work stations, response time and a host of other computer criteria. IT is tangible. Information is a less tangible resource. It could be defined as 'data that has been evaluated for some use'.

Creating strategic change

Some businesses have used IT to gain and hold strategic advantage whereas others have simply employed better use of their existing information resources to strengthen their position. Both are packaged together under the IT label, but there are important differences. The case of a company that locks in its customers by the placing of computer terminals in each customer location to allow easy order placement and to provide up-to-date pricing and accounts information comes to mind. As a result, the customer now finds it more difficult and less attractive to change suppliers. This change has been effected by the technology, not the information that the company supplied; the technology has given the company's information extra value. Another company may be contemplating an expansion programme through acquisition. It purchases access to a commercial database for likely takeover targets and is thus using new information to create a strategic change.

There are many instances in which a company will make use of both the technology and the information. Imagine an airline that places terminals in the offices of hundreds of travel agents so that it can run its reservation system with a competitive advantage. It then uses the information that it has assembled on various routes and alters some of its discount-seat pricing, enabling it to hold a larger share of a volatile low-priced seat market. The final payout may be when the airline decides to sell some of this information to other carriers, allowing it to generate income and reinforce its public image as an innovator. It can retain its competitive edge by deciding precisely how much of its data it is prepared to let the competition have.

Cost of information

Information-related activities now represent one of the biggest single costs in any company. It is no longer just a matter of producing information, but of storing and archiving it (no one seems to destroy information). Again our 'accounting mentality' has often prevented us from recognising this and actively doing something about it. If information is defined as 'knowledge for the purpose of taking effective action', an easy causal relationship is established at the outset. Data, or undigested information, may be cheap and easy to produce because of the power of today's computer technology, but it only becomes of real value to a company if that data/information can be assimilated by individuals and put to good corporate use.

The IT industry may soon have to refocus its attention to the ease of assimilation of information rather than the simple presentation of bald words and numbers on two-colour screens. Otherwise executives run **Overloads** the risk of information overload. Information assistants, executive information systems and improved user interfaces will all have an important role to play in ensuring that information supports the organisation rather than swamps it.

An important feature of information within an organisation is that most of it – perhaps up to 80 per cent – remains local and stays within the confines of a small group of people. Successive filtering permits only a trickle of information reaching the next tier of management. Sometimes this is what is needed to manage the business, sometimes it is not. Information filtering will become less easy as managers begin to make greater use of multiple information channels to cross-check their sources of information.

Different countries seek different benefits

Across the EC, attitudes towards IT vary and managements in different countries expect different levels of performance and return on investment. The rationale behind IT investments is no longer predominantly cost saving as was the case in the early 1980s. There has been a growing emphasis on investments that improve customer service, managerial effectiveness and staff productivity.

In France, improved customer service is the most cited benefit that management hopes to derive from IT and recently there has been a sudden switch to improving managerial effectiveness, which formerly was not considered a top priority. French IT efforts in product quality have also taken great strides recently. For French management as a whole, the most crucial areas of IT investment are executive decision support, office automation, electronic trading links, replacing out-dated systems and spreading the use of electronic point-of-sale (EPOS) technology.

West German management tends to look at cost–benefit equations when examining IT projects. Staff productivity is one of their main concerns and most investment emphasis is given to office automation, followed by executive decision support, replacing outdated systems, computer-integrated manufacturing (CIM) and internal telecommunications.

In the UK, the IT emphasis is on better customer service, managerial effectiveness and gaining competitive advantage. To this end, UK management is focusing on replacing outdated systems, installing adequate decision support facilities, upgrading office automation and internal administration and establishing electronic trading links.

The Italians have been less adventurous with IT and their prime goals are to improve overall managerial effectiveness and their competitive position. Office automation and executive decision support are also important features of Italian IT strategies.

Customers benefit from information-oriented companies

Knowledge of customer requirements is vital if companies are to target the right products to the right markets. Some companies, especially in the financial services area, are trying to go further to build a more complete picture of individual customers from the variety of transactions they engage in. IT suppliers, for example, and service oriented companies are seeking to go beyond individual transactions to build on-going relationships with their major customers. The information gathered helps supplier and customer alike. Case studies of both the airline industry and the banking industry reveal similar experiences with handling people and information.

Airline industry

In the airline industry, the different airlines' product is largely the same: aircraft from a handful of aerospace manufacturers, similar seat design and baggage handling, similar journey times and safety standards. The more the operations became similar, the greater became the need to differentiate between the airlines. Some carriers tried to build up a special relationship with the customer and move him/her beyond the single transaction level. A wide variety of innovations were tried, such as special promotions, segregation of different classes, frequent flyer programmes, complete non-smoking aircraft and total smoking aircraft. At the end of the day, it was hoped that the passenger would differentiate between the similar products on the basis of these other factors.

Banking industry

The banking industry, likewise, invested millions establishing efficient and secure transaction networks. Being early and large-scale users of computer technology, the banks were able to deliver cheap and reliable account services, but they did not discover the need to go for the 'whole person' approach until quite late. Their entry into the mortgage market was hesitant and not uniformly successful. Their movement into the building societies' traditional preserve did not go unchallenged. Societies quickly realised that the banks could erode valuable layers of their business unless they responded in kind.

The hand-written building society passbook became a thing of the past. 'Hole-in-the-wall' cash dispensers accompanied new shop fronts and carefully designed corporate images. They turned the tables on the banks by offering banking services such as current accounts, and used co-operative ventures in the delivery of new electronic services to achieve economies of scale. Most importantly they were also able to generate economies of scale by widespread merger, a development that had taken place in the banking industry decades previously. The banks' rigid computer infrastructure had turned into a liability rather than an asset. Competitive advantage had been won and then lost. Information systems are now used extensively by banks and building societies alike to retain and gain market share.

Improving management effectiveness

By using a variety of techniques, ranging from assessing information flows and volumes, communication styles and patterns, to data entities and architectures, it is possible to build an 'information profile' of an organisation. This has many advantages:

- Recognition of what is corporate, divisional and individual information

- Recognition of what information must be shared and at what levels within the organisation

- Identification and quantification of the effort and cost of maintaining the various information bases

- Recognition of the value information has or should bring to the organisation

- A framework for decision making on individual projects

While some organisations agree on the need for an IT strategy, fewer see the need to develop a similar strategy for the information itself. If we see IT as one of the building components of a company's activities, information is the cement that comes in contact with all the other blocks and binds them together. The strength of the corporate edifice will be determined by the quality of each of the blocks and of the cement which keeps them in place.

Computers and the business world

In the space of forty years, computers and IT have transformed modern society. A great deal of the world's corporate activity is now tied directly or indirectly to the manufacture, service, support and use of computer technology. No business organisation can escape the use of IT in some form.

3. The world IT scene

'Europe is not the ideal place for the development of cutting-edge information technology' *Vittorio Cassoni, chief executive of Olivetti*

'Europe has not disappeared from the information technology map, we are still in the game' *Jean Marie Cadiou, head of ESPRIT*

The state of IT in the Community is summed up in these two comments. Cassoni stresses that Europe cannot hope to be in the vanguard of IT developments because the domestic markets are too small and that the USA will continue to provide the lead. Cadiou is realistic enough to know that unless strenuous efforts are made to develop domestic Community IT, European manufacturers will stumble and fall in the face of future global IT competition. Figure 7 illustrates the relative size of US and Japanese IT companies by 1987 revenue while Figure 8 shows the size of the different national electronics markets in 1986.

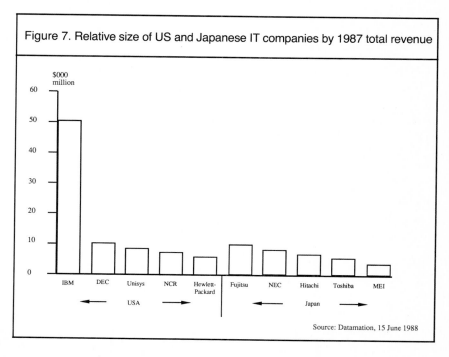

Figure 7. Relative size of US and Japanese IT companies by 1987 total revenue

Source: Datamation, 15 June 1988

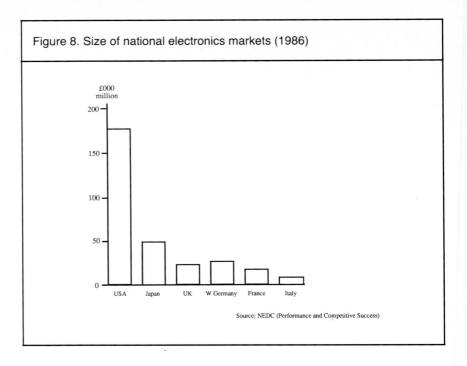

Figure 8. Size of national electronics markets (1986)

Source: NEDC (Performance and Competitive Success)

The world scene

The world IT industry is dominated by three US and three Japanese companies. International Business Machines (IBM) is the largest with almost 25 per cent of the world's information systems market, while the others – Digital (DEC), Unisys, Fujitsu, NEC and Hitachi – hold market shares of about 5 per cent each. These companies concentrate largely on the manufacture of computer hardware.

- The UK's largest IT company – STC – holds about 1 per cent of the world market

- No single supplier holds more than 5 per cent of the world software and services market and most software firms are small but innovative

The UK has only one domestic mainframe producer, but it has had many successes with high quality and creative software firms. The nation's strengths in IT lie in the universal use of the English language, staff mobility and its good track record for major systems developments. We should be well placed to exploit these advantages. However, several of the biggest EC software companies are French and foreign software companies have made significant inroads into the UK market.

The Japanese, US and European IT industries are mutually dependent, with Europe's IT companies relying on the USA and Japan for the design and supply of basic electronic components and for operating systems. The UK is the third largest IT market in the world but it is dwarfed by both the USA and Japan. Current growth rates in the European IT market of 20 per cent per annum are forecast to fall to between 10 and 15 per cent during the next decade, although the IT services industry, worth an estimated £2 billion annually, will see growth rates of up to 30 per cent a year.

The IT market in the EC is likely to suffer radical changes because of 1992 and the force of Japanese and US competition. The current IT market in Europe is dominated by IBM, the leading US mainframe manufacturer, which has about 19 per cent of total sales by value. Siemens is the only European IT company to have an EC market share of as much as 5 per cent:

IT in Europe
(1987 market share %)

IBM	19
Siemens	5
DEC	4
Olivetti	4
Bull	3
Nixdorf	3
Unisys	3
Philips	2
HP	2

The structure of the EC IT market is clarified further if one looks at the importance of the four key domestic players in the EC market (Figure 9). West Germany is the dominant IT nation with 26 per cent of the total $100 billion market that existed in 1987, while the UK is the next most important with a 20 per cent share. France comes third with a 17 per cent share and Italy fourth with 11 per cent.

The business work-station market is dominated by IBM, Olivetti, Amstrad and Apple, while Digital, Hewlett-Packard and NCR (through sourcing arrangements) hold the dominant positions in the mini-computer market. ICL and Olivetti are also beginning to do well with their UNIX ranges of departmental servers.

Most US companies rely to a large extent on the European market for a large portion of their sales. Europe as a region may represent only

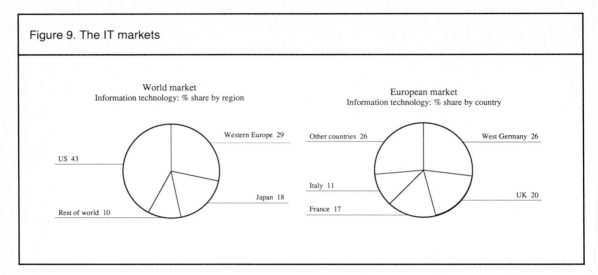

Figure 9. The IT markets

World market
Information technology: % share by region

US 43
Western Europe 29
Japan 18
Rest of world 10

European market
Information technology: % share by country

Other countries 26
West Germany 26
Italy 11
France 17
UK 20

29 per cent of the world's entire IT market (compared with the USA's 43 per cent), but it will continue to be a bloody battleground for international vendors in future decades.

European computer sales
(as % of total)

Amstrad	49
Nixdorf★	40
Olivetti★	35
IBM	31
NCR	31
HP	27
Unisys	26
DEC	24
STC	13

★ excluding UK

Barriers to the exploitation of technology

Despite the growth of IT as a vital ingredient in modern business, there have been a number of technical, and some artificial, barriers to its wider use. Some typical barriers are:

● Incompatible, multi-vendor environments

● Hierarchical and proprietary networks

- High cost of ownership

- Inability to move data between applications and databases

- Confusing variety of 'unfriendly' user interfaces

These would normally be sufficient to stifle any attempts to introduce new technology, but matters have been made worse by managerial practices:

- Information management separated from operations environment

- Narrow view of strategic potential and investment returns

- Lack of company-wide information flows

- Organisational and cultural barriers to teamwork

Many of these problems are examined at length in subsequent chapters.

Harmonisation of standards

IT customers have been aware of the need for standardised computer systems and have started the slow move towards harmonisation of standards. There has been a parallel realisation by IT vendors that they must try to standardise as much of what is within their control as possible, otherwise they will not be able to achieve the economies of scale they need. Even at the most basic level, the task is enormous. There is no such thing as a standard European PABX, while some companies seem to take a perverse delight in the virtues of one television broadcasting standard over another.

Even a QWERTY keyboard layout has to become AZERTY in France and QWERTZ in West Germany. It will be some time early in the next century before manufacturers reach any agreement on basic common commands such as the 'shift/control' button on a keyboard. The lack of any cohesive framework of standards within the computer industry stems from its rapid development over the past four decades. It has been part of the nature of the computer industry to introduce changes faster than organisations can cope.

Declining competitiveness in Europe

Insufficient spending on research

The European Commission has been concerned that levels of IT research and development spending within the EC may not be sufficient to give European industry the backbone necessary to compete in the 1990s. The Commission has estimated that *per capita* spending on

IT research in Europe is £28.50, while Japan spends about £42 per person and the USA £72. In absolute terms, however, European expenditure of £8.5 billion on IT research and development is substantially higher than total Japanese expenditure of £4.6 billion. The USA, which spends almost £16 billion annually on IT research and development, exceeds the combined Japanese and EC totals.

Although IT research and development in the EC may be greater than that in Japan, it is more fragmented and spread over a large number of competing organisations and countries. Duplication of effort has meant less effective use of the research funds. Furthermore the relationship between expenditure and gross domestic product (GDP) is illuminating. Since 1981, the USA, Japan, West Germany and France have increased their R&D/GDP ratios while the UK ratio has declined. The IT markets are growing in most EC member states but European manufacturers are not necessarily expanding their market share in line with this growth (Figure 10).

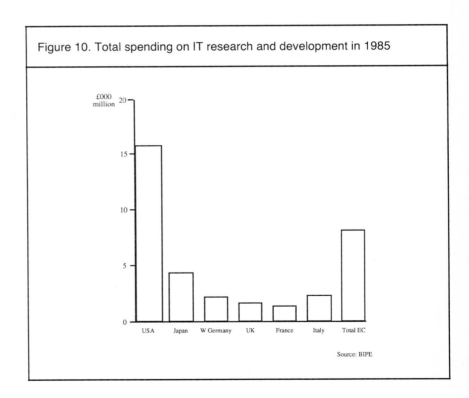

Figure 10. Total spending on IT research and development in 1985

Source: BIPE

European co-operation

ESPRIT

A single market has already been in operation for five years in European IT research and development, albeit on a small scale. In 1984, the Commission set up the 3 billion ecu (£2.1 billion) collaborative programme known as ESPRIT (European Strategic Programme for Research in Information Technology). Five years later, it is regarded as a showpiece of Community technology policy. In the words of its chairman, it kept the Community on the IT map.

Esprit was set three targets by the Commission:

● To encourage cross-border co-operation

● To develop new technologies

● To create pan-European IT standards

The project has been very successful in helping to stem the tide of European alliances with US companies. Cross-border IT alliances within the EC numbered only six in 1983 but had jumped to forty-six by 1986. EC–US alliances have also increased but at a slower rate: from thirty-two in 1983 to forty-nine in 1986. The net result of this is that the EC has reduced its dependence on IT from the USA and now relies more on indigenous R&D.

Industrial robots

In standards, ESPRIT has created Communications Network for Manufacturing Applications (CNMA) which allows different kinds of industrial robots to work side by side in an automated factory. It has gone beyond much of the work that General Motors achieved with its Manufacturing Automation Protocol (MAP) standard. The immediate impact of CNMA is that it reduces the chance that a company installing a new automated production line will have to choose US or Japanese products. It provides an EC alternative and increases the size of the factory automation market in the Community.

Document transfer

Another ESPRIT project, Office Document Architecture (ODA), is a collaborative venture between Olivetti, Siemens, Bull and ICL, designed to allow document transfer from one type of desk-top computer to another. ODA has already been accepted by the International Standards Institute.

The great significance of ESPRIT is that it deals with pre-competitive R&D. Trans-national consortia are formed to make specific project proposals, funding for which is split between the EC and the sponsoring organisations. One of ESPRIT's main achievements has been in fostering trans-national and industry–academia collaboration. It is frequently the case that companies which have collaborated in ESPRIT think first of each other when seeking help in new technological or geographical markets, and that they look beyond their local universities for basic research. EC industry has discovered that there are world-class IT research groups in Belgium, Greece, the Republic of Ireland and Portugal, despite the lack of an IT industry in these countries.

Global standards

The complexity of many large modern organisations has forced them to consider setting standards of quality, service and communications to which individual units of the company can adhere and which will allow suppliers to conform to specification more easily, thereby enabling them to develop a long-term business relationship.

General Motors, the world's largest manufacturer, has over 40,000 intelligent machines in use for design and manufacturing operations. They include computer systems, robots and programmable controllers. General Motors estimates, however, that only 15 per cent of these machines can communicate with other systems and that up to 50 per cent of the cost of installing new automation is spent on allowing one computer to speak to another.

MAP
General Motors has been pressing for standard methods of communicating between systems and gave its suppliers a deadline by which their systems should conform to MAP. What General Motors hopes to achieve is a compatibility of systems not only within the company but with other organisations as well. MAP and other protocols are the first steps in building global IT networks. MAP relates to local area networks, namely communication between systems on one site rather than over telephone lines. MAP currently defines standards for:

- Physical connections, such as the cables to link systems

- Data link protocol, which would prevent systems that shared a network from corrupting one another's data

- Transport protocol, such as controlling how systems send simultaneous signals through a network

General Motors hopes to extend MAP to other aspects of networking and has been encouraged by the endorsement of the standard by IBM, Digital, Hewlett-Packard and Motorola. Boeing is now attempting to create a similar standard for its engineering department with its Technical Office Protocol. Early experiences of these standards indicate that the cost of implementation is still very high.

Dramatic developments towards a new industry-wide technical open systems standard have taken place within the past eighteen months. The origins of open systems lie in the early 1970s when **UNIX** AT&T's Bell Laboratories produced a standard operating system for minicomputers called UNIX. In recent years, this system has been licensed with more than twenty versions of it offered as options by all the leading computer manufacturers. Some analysts have estimated that sales of UNIX computers reached $8 billion in 1987 and are likely to exceed $25 billion within five years.

When AT&T announced in 1987 that it was to produce a merged UNIX that could act as an industry standard, reactions were generally favourable since the US telecommunications group had little vested interest in promoting this standard. In October 1987, AT&T revealed that it would develop the merged UNIX in partnership with Sun Microsystems, the fastest growing hardware manufacturer in the USA. General opinion in the computer industry was that this move would give Sun at least a one-year lead over its rivals. AT&T in effect threw down the gauntlet in January 1988 by announcing that it was buying a 20 per cent stake in Sun for $250 million spread over three years. The competitive edge was no longer confined to Sun but extended to AT&T.

Computer industry rivals objected and hastily mounted a challenge. By March this had taken the form of Digital, Hewlett-Packard and Apollo Computer deciding to establish the Open Software Foundation, a non-profit, jointly financed organisation to develop their own industry-wide standards. Their ranks were soon joined by Siemens, Bull, Nixdorf and IBM. These seven companies authorised a $90 million budget to come up with their own brand of UNIX within **POSIX** eighteen months and to look at the possibility of a standard interface system, POSIX, which can allow software to run on any system.

The race is on, although there may be only one winner – the user. UNIX may not polarise into two camps but, if it does, the interface standards do not differ greatly and there may be room for both versions of UNIX. The feeling in the industry generally is that two closely aligned standards are infinitely better than dozens of proprietary standards.

These developments in UNIX and network management have taken place against the backdrop of developments in Open Systems **Open Systems** Interconnection (OSI). The OSI concept was created in 1978 when the **Interconnection** International Standards Organisation began developing a new architecture and group of protocols designed for the emerging distributed information and telecommunications systems. By 1986, a set of seven-layer specifications was published. Significantly, these OSI rules are supported by all the major suppliers including IBM, Digital, Unisys, NCR and ICL. Whereas some vendors, such as ICL and Unisys, have incorporated the OSI spirit deep into their designs, IBM has retained proprietary networking systems for connection between its own products but provides a special software 'bridge' to link with OSI-based systems. Only recently has IBM exhibited public interest in the promotion of open systems, as a second string to their proprietary bow.

Of LANs, WANs and VANs

One of the immediate benefits of the OSI standards was the creation of local area networks (LANs) and wide area networks (WANs). A LAN can consist of a single building, a large industrial complex or a university campus that may be spread over several square kilometres. Local area networking is effective in moving information economically over short distances at high speeds and with high levels of accuracy. The most popular LAN standard is Ethernet (otherwise known as ISO 8802/3 or IEEE 802.3), developed for general office, retail, banking and factory use. A recent study concluded that current local area networking technology was sufficiently advanced to boost the productivity of a small department of twenty-five managers and secretaries by 10 per cent because of the improvement in communications.

Wide area networks (WANs) offer inter-site and off-site communication on a national or international basis. One of the most obvious aspects of wide area networking is the development of electronic mail, which is increasingly operated on the basis of the X.400 international standard for handling messages. Both LANs and WANs are the building blocks of electronic data interchange (EDI), which has been used for some years to underpin the paperless trading between commercial organisations. Various communications protocols have been used to carry EDI messages but there is a growing trend for X.400 protocols as the communications base.

A further step along the network route is the value-added network (VAN). Since 1986 there have been significant developments in the EC regulatory environment. In a number of member states, reorganisation of domestic telecommunications has taken place or is due shortly and the Commission has issued a Green Paper outlining, among other things, a timetable for the deregulation of VANs. But definitions of deregulation, competition and VANs can vary from country to country. The UK, which has the most developed VANs market, mainly because it was the first to liberalise, plans further changes. In West Germany, major changes are planned which should permit a free market for data service provision, although the federal nature of the country dictates that local state views may need to be accommodated at a later stage. A French government decree in 1987 permitted considerable freedom in the provision of VANs, provided that the 'value-added' content of the service accounts for at least 85 per cent of the tariff and that the transport element accounts for no more than 15 per cent.

Italian telecommunications are heavily influenced by political events which will determine the precise shape of the eventual merger of SIP, Italcable and ASST into one company, although the dividing line between private- and public-sector activities may not be as clear as some observers hope. Spain created a new VANs framework in 1987 that allows Telefonica to retain its monopoly in basic and mobile telephony, videotext and teletext, while other services will be open to competition. Sweden, Norway and the Republic of Ireland are beginning to liberalise their sectors while the Netherlands has a VANs regime as progressive as that in the UK. Belgian telecommunications, on the other hand, remain conservative.

A number of VANs operate across Europe, while some VAN services are available across several public networks. The freedom created in the single market will make it easier for national VAN operators wishing to operate a pan-European service. Complexity of tariff structures is one area that needs to be examined since VAN traffic will span more than one country. Ideally, a German customer accessing a UK VAN will pay the same as a French subscriber to the same service. It will be up to the VAN operators and national public telephone and telegraph authorities to apportion the revenues.

Moves towards open systems take hold

From the business point of view, one of the most important innovations in the computer industry in recent years has been the trend towards international standards. Partly as a result of pressure from the Commission and partly as a result of various national agencies' purchasing power, there has been a growing recognition of the importance of open, international standards in systems procurement.

Suppliers have responded to these calls with vocal support for open standards and networks while continuing to offer their proprietary solutions to business problems. There have also been the competing

UNIX developments described above. The hapless purchaser of an IT system is therefore faced with a bewildering choice not only between competing proprietary solutions but between proprietary and open systems.

There are various reasons why proprietary systems are not going to disappear overnight:

- They have already made huge contributions to corporate profitability and organisational effectiveness

- Major proprietary networks support key business functions and because of their structure will grow in importance

- Much of their usefulness has not yet been exploited

- A range of corporate alliances has developed to meet future demand and market requirements

Nevertheless, the case for open systems is clear-cut. Open systems free the user from dependence on a particular computer vendor.

Benefits of open systems

To appreciate the benefits that open systems offer, it is necessary to look at three areas:

- Technical

- Economic

- Political

The technical dimension

There has been a growing awareness of the importance of IT to overall business performance and this has forced a more active concern with the total IT architecture of an organisation. If different divisions or departments have different and incompatible technologies, a company runs the risk of creating artificial barriers to exploiting the technology to the full. Similarly, if there have been different development paths for the centralised data-processing system, the departmental applications and office systems, and the personal and professional computer systems, it may prove impossible to bring these together into a coherent framework.

The attraction of an open technical architecture that could subsume these differences is obvious. Anyone setting up a company today would opt for such an architecture. Technically it allows a software framework to be developed which corresponds to the open technical architecture and allows a company to standardise those components that it deems necessary. These may include fourth generation language, relational databases, information retrieval and office systems.

An organisation can also standardise on the user interface it considers most appropriate for its business. Extensive development work will be necessary in this area but the demand for a solution to incompatible user interfaces within and between applications is very real. The real problem is for organisations which already have proprietary architecture in place. Much work remains to be done on finding a way, let alone an easy way, to move from a series of discrete proprietary architectures to a coherent open architecture.

The economic dimension

An open systems approach makes use of widely available hardware or software components. A company can shop around and negotiate the lowest possible cost. Documented universal standards also mean that many companies can write software and sell it to a potentially huge market. This has the effect of driving costs down and widening the range of software products. Open systems will minimise the overheads of supporting multiple different systems both for the information systems department and for user training, once the organisation has lived through the transition period.

The political dimension

Customer gains control

The most powerful argument in favour of an open systems architecture is that it turns the tables on the IT suppliers and gives control back to the customer. With any proprietary system, the customer is dependent on the supplier's strategy for developments. Put more bluntly, the customer's success depends on the success of the computer company. If the supplier decides to change planned developments or alter priorities, the customer is helpless. With open systems, the market potential is larger and no single vendor will dominate. The customers will be able to play one vendor off against another to guarantee value for money and quality service. Another important political benefit is that changes can take place within an evolutionary framework. The overall open systems framework provides guidance and limits to what can be achieved, and allows an organisation greater flexibility in its use of systems. Open systems can be relocated, if necessary, within the organisation.

Open systems simplify the procurement process. Instead of having to go through a lengthy procedure of matching requirements against what suppliers are offering, the focus is on using standard components to achieve the business functionality that is needed.

The politics of 'Who's first?'

There is widespread support for open systems in theory, but few companies seem prepared to take the necessary first steps in planning the transition. What is necessary is a change in the thinking of those within the organisation and a gradual change in corporate philosophy towards open IT systems.

One of the obstacles to organisations taking the necessary steps forward is the belief that IT will become an 'either/or' world where existing proprietary systems and the next generation of open systems are mutually exclusive. It is more sensible to view future IT developments as embracing both types of system. They will have to live beside each other for years and their interfaces and inter-relationships will need clarification.

There are three main objections to developing open systems within a particular organisation:

- Technical objections

- Market factors

- Human and organisational considerations

Technical objections

The biggest single technical reservation about open systems is lack of experience. The area is complex and the progress towards achieving the desired standards is relatively slow. Managers need to be convinced that promises will be honoured, otherwise it means placing an inordinate amount of faith in a relatively small number of technicians who will set the new standards.

Another problem is justifying the move to a new standard after so much has been invested in the existing proprietary system. It is easy for a new company starting from scratch, but for most companies the stakes are very high. Equally, concern centres on the quality of the systems available within the open system framework. Do they match the functionality, completeness and reliability of the proprietary products? Will the quality of implementation match existing proprietary suppliers and will the standards-making process keep pace with technological innovation?

Another problem is who to blame if things do not work. By using proprietary systems, a customer knows precisely where he should point an accusing finger if delivery dates or quality levels are not met. It may prove more difficult to know which part of a multi-vendor system is at fault.

And, finally, there are variations of UNIX being promoted by different supplier groups. In this crucial area of uniformity, international agreement is lacking. It is unclear whether the so-called Archer Group of UNIX International or the Open Software Foundation will become the international standard.

Many of these objections are valid. Open system functionality can be limited. There are shortages of skills and experience and it requires the customer to manage the inter-relationship between the various hardware and software vendors. It also requires managing additional and different systems during the transition. These concerns boil down to asking whether the benefits outweigh the costs. The answer will be different for each company depending on what systems it already has, to what extent it wants IT to support its business drive, and to what degree it wants to be in the driving seat with its IT developments.

Market factors

Since the number of installed open systems is relatively small, it may prove difficult to project how rapidly the market will grow. Unless there is a huge growth in demand, open systems will not be able to achieve the vital economies of scale that proprietary systems have achieved. Market research projections have been grossly inaccurate in forecasting recent IT developments: the success of videotext was greatly over-estimated while the appeal of cellular radio was grossly under-estimated. If a viable open systems market does not develop, the necessary infrastructure, skills and software will be found wanting, and open systems will have proved to be another brief, if dazzling, challenger to the supremacy of the proprietary vendors.

IT's track record has been uneven and uncertain as far as growth is concerned. IT development by its very nature is volatile and unpredictable. Over forty years, the industry has generated and accommodated a number of paradigm shifts that have effectively forced wholesale rethinking of everything that went before it. Valves were followed by transistors and semi-conductors. Open systems are as fundamental a change as any of these. The path of IT away from centralised solutions towards flexible solutions has required many brave decisions to be taken by managements unclear as to how future technological trends would develop.

The only way to survive in this uncertain environment is to monitor the progress of open systems and match that progression with the right resources. If progress is slow, investment in planning and transition should be modest; if progress is more rapid than expected, a company may find itself at a competitive disadvantage if it does not keep pace with developments.

Human and organisational considerations

Resistance to change

Few people like change and most organisations have major problems in managing change. Resistance to the changes that open systems bring about will be both passive and active as people attempt to defend systems that they had a role in introducing or supporting. Some may even take it personally. Emphasis should be placed on weakening the opposition to open systems rather than on promoting them aggressively, as this may lead to fresh resistance.

The situation requires an atmosphere in which change will be considered positive. Such an atmosphere will be created by:

- An emphasis on job security

- A commitment to the enhancement of skills

- Adequate support for people during transition

- A clear statement that open systems are worthy of investigation and may be important for the future

- Encouragement for change and innovation elsewhere in the organisation

Developing an open systems strategy

When an organisation is developing an open systems information and technology (OSIT) strategy, it must pose the same questions and make the same analysis of business objectives as when it is developing any other kind of IT strategy. While an OSIT strategy also needs the same kind of agreement between the board and the information system department on how to develop the business strategy, it differs from the conventional IT strategy in its recognition and acceptance that the IT world is moving towards an open systems environment.

The organisation therefore *seeks* open systems solutions, or platforms that will evolve into open systems, rather than accepting a single supplier's proprietary solution to their business problems. They do this because they believe the open platform will provide them with a more robust, resilient and flexible route.

Open systems will not necessarily be the immediate foundation of an organisation's IT networking, but organisations will need to plan for an effective transition between proprietary and non-proprietary systems. Each organisation must choose its own route and lay effective plans.

It will need to plan the technical framework for open systems and to address the 'process of change'. It needs to determine:

- What style of innovation it wants

- How much effort it will make to sell this change to end-users

- What level of involvement there will be for those affected by the change

Technology a two-edged sword

Most people and organisations work on the naive assumption that technological change will automatically be good. The advent of steam and the printed word brought with them social disruption, mass upheaval and huge personal changes. In the information industry, the only thing that an increase in data is guaranteed to produce is more stress. Companies can find themselves trapped by the volumes of data that they have generated and unable to act on any of it.

Technology is never neutral in the impact it has on people's working lives. It can harm or it can enhance the quality of work that people do. The important thing that companies must recognise is that technology will have an impact on the organisation and it is up to them to ensure that the effect will be positive rather than negative. Active and high-level management of the IT resource will be something many companies will have to get to grips with.

4. Building the business strategy

Drivers for change

For practical strategists, what are the main effects of the 1992 single market? The 'drivers for change', those issues and trends which cause businesses to re-appraise and perhaps change their business directions, are as follows:

- De-regulation will create freedom for changes in consumer behaviour

- Market behaviour will alter as new distribution channels open up for products and services

- Competitors will react to the changes in the market sectors they share with your business and will extend their horizons to admit new approaches to their business strategy

Anticipate changes

A brief evaluation of these three drivers will indicate whether 1992 has a significance for your business or not. Do not, however, waste resources at this stage on trying to find out *exactly* which directives could affect you, how and when. The important thing is to be ready to change direction to deal with the changes before they affect you, not *as* they happen.

But these are only part of the picture. To the 1992 drivers must be added:

- Demographic trends

- Technology trends (including IT)

- Economic trends

- Political trends

These last two, particularly, will have a profound effect on business strategy. European economies and politics will still have an existence outside 1992 single market considerations. Regional economies will dictate much of the market opportunities. Companies have to ask themselves whether they will be impacted by any of these seven trends. If they answer 'yes' or 'don't know', they have to revisit their present business strategy.

The choices

Executives may not always be in the best position to review current strategy. Senior managers have to be prepared to question the status quo, especially where they have been involved in establishing the working methods and procedures. The basic problem for many UK companies is that there is often no formally stated strategy. Even worse, there are strategic components (like revenue/profitability targets) which are not supported by any strategic action plans whatever.

This leaves the business vulnerable when fundamental questions like, 'Should we respond to 1992 and if so, how?' are asked. Very few companies in Europe have a formal strategy. This gives your company a major opportunity to achieve competitive advantage through the formulation and implementation of a good 'European' strategy. The implementation will involve a number of discrete steps, and the overall strategy must be flexible enough to encompass unexpected opportunities (Figure 11).

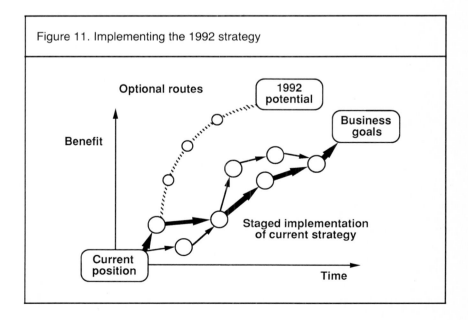

Figure 11. Implementing the 1992 strategy

Developing a 1992 strategy

This brings us to the first choice, do we invest in developing a coherent strategy or not? Before you rush enthusiastically into the 'yes' choices, there are a few sobering considerations which have to be faced:

- 'Are you prepared to wait six months for a result?' Few worthwhile advantages ever emerge in a shorter time frame.

- 'Is the top team prepared to devote the time input required to develop a strategic plan?' Many strategic plans fail because the top team does not put in sufficient time to develop and understand them.

- 'Can you accept that most of the information which you need has to be collected systematically?' External data collection is often neglected. If this happens it is at the expense of the strategy.

If you are not in a position to deliver on each of these – timescale, input and data – then do not start. What the management textbooks do not tell you is that you can have a successful business without a formal strategy. If the effort involved for you to develop a strategy is at this time too diversionary do not do it. You can take initiatives and 'chunk' your business forward in the best traditions of corporate development. You will feel the absence of a coherent strategy however when:

- You seek a way of unifying the initiatives

- You try to identify the priorities for attention and resources

- You consider if your customers, markets or even business are vulnerable to a competitor – UK, European, or global

The 1992 Response Matrix has been developed to categorise four generic responses to the single market (Figure 12).

Offensive and defensive strategies

The offensive business

The offensive business cannot wait to get into Europe. The company bulges with entrepreneurial zeal and is viewed by its competitors as a market leader. It has an overview of what the unified market is and it is prepared to revamp its entire corporate strategy, marketing, and even its organisational structure in order to cope with the changes that 1992

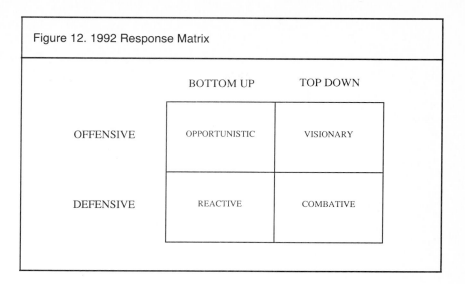

Figure 12. 1992 Response Matrix

	BOTTOM UP	TOP DOWN
OFFENSIVE	OPPORTUNISTIC	VISIONARY
DEFENSIVE	REACTIVE	COMBATIVE

will bring about. It has already been successful in its traditional markets and now seeks further marketing opportunities in the EC for its existing products. But it is also prepared to examine what products it must make to satisfy European demand.

The defensive business

The defensive company views the EC as a threat. It will do only what is necessary to maintain its current market position and head off inroads made by competitors. Defensive companies abound in traditionally weak industries and sectors and have faced little competition or change in demand for years. Long-term strategies, if they exist, are often unclear or out of date. It has no vision of a unified Europe. Instead it assesses aspects of EC legislation one by one. If the company needs to comply with new EC regulations, it will do so only gradually. The defensive company hopes to hold its domestic market share in the face of EC competition while it is attempting to restructure its own industry.

The response model illustrates the range of possible reaction to major strategic events such as the advent of the single market. The response may be from the bottom upwards in which case the company will attempt to meet the EC challenge to its own industry slowly and piecemeal, whereas the top-down approach will focus on the basic principle of the single market and look at the impact of this on a company-wide basis, affecting all aspects of the business at once.

Assuming you have chosen to revisit your strategy and formulate a new one, the matrix identifies a visionary response as being the most effective a business can provide. Why?

The visionary and opportunistic responses both see 1992 as an opportunity. The visionary approach identifies opportunity for creating new business based on long-term, sustainable competitive advantage. This approach is only possible where it is driven from the top, since it needs to call on resources from many parts of the company.

Where response is left to junior and middle management, it tends to concentrate on immediate opportunities created by individual directives. This response is not necessarily based on underlying company strengths or market changes, and is vulnerable to competitor initiatives.

The same top-down and bottom-up approaches differentiate the combative and reactive responses by those companies for whom 1992 is a threat. This difference in approach is between companies who realise they can influence the future, and plan effectively to do so; and companies who either feel they are at the mercy of fate, or who fail to plan their response.

Managing both internal and external perspectives

The environment in which management will have to deal with 1992-related change is unevenly divided into internal and external components. Managerial control can be secured over corporate R&D strategy, people, systems and technology. Within this internal environment, the strategy will reflect a wide number of intangible elements that lead to the corporate vision of the future. Less influence is exercised over the external market and the products that the company must make for this market.

The impact of 1992 on competitive position

The implications of a single market add an extra level of complexity to many already highly complicated business structures. Many industries will change dramatically while others will be affected only in a minor way; it is therefore important for a company to question how 1992 will affect them before rushing blindly into an unnecessary pan-European strategy.

Understand your competitive position

At the root of this is the importance of understanding the 'competitive position' of a company. Companies that are currently underperforming in the domestic market are more than likely to underperform in a European market, regardless of the expansion strategy they might adopt. It is, therefore, crucial for a company to understand its current competitive position and to know what are the key driving forces of change in its industry; only then can it develop a business strategy and the IT strategy which complements it.

1992 will be a watershed for UK companies – they will be faced with a market six times greater than their own and one which accounts for 23 per cent of world gross national product. They will be exposed to fierce competition and will be forced to relearn fundamental knowledge they have taken for granted in their own market.

The first five years

The pace of change within the EC over the next decade will be intense. It is crucial that companies are well positioned as the single market nears completion to gain the benefits of the exponential growth. The first five years of the new market will provide enormous competitive advantage compared with earlier or later periods. This S-curve must be caught on the rapid ascent (Figure 13). As the strategies are being developed, management must identify and establish critical success factors – the milestones along a company's journey, which indicate how far the company is from its ultimate destination.

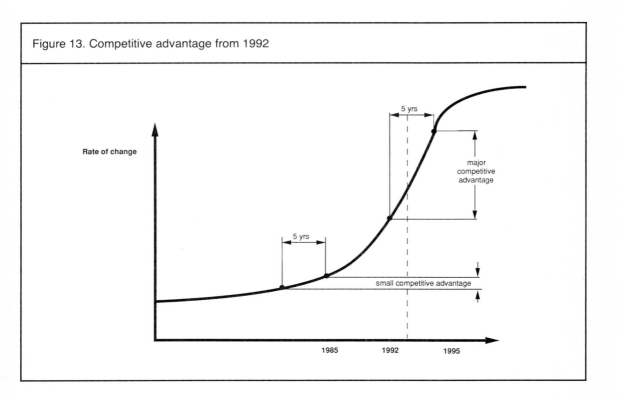

Figure 13. Competitive advantage from 1992

Business strategy, IT strategy and customer needs

To be a winning company in Europe, a company must:

- Be aware of the strategic dimensions of the single market

- Be alert to the weaknesses of simplistic strategic responses to 1992 opportunities and threats

- Place the IT strategy in an overall business strategy context

- Link IT initiatives to winning in Europe through the enhancement of strategic business advantage

All of these factors must be driven by 'customer needs'. Customer needs are not an abstract concept. They are the core business value. As Levitt, the Harvard marketing guru, puts it: 'The purpose of a business is to create and keep a customer.' Whether it is doughnuts or diesels, this simple fact remains true. However, to get the capital to run the business, the company needs to attract and retain funds by increasing the business's value to the shareholders. This is the central objective of a business strategy. To keep creating and retaining a customer requires sustained competitive advantage over a period. So three simple concepts should be sufficient to drive the business strategy:

- Creating and keeping a customer

- Increasing shareholder value

- Competitive advantage

What is the European challenge, then? It is about:

- Creating new European customers

- Keeping existing customers

- Increasing the value of the business in a new European context

- Seeking new ways of achieving competitive advantage

Information technology is relevant to all of these.

We must not, however, overlook the non-Europeans who are attracted to the EC in increasing numbers. European companies are vulnerable to this interest. As Sir John Harvey-Jones has pointed out, the industry structures of the USA and Japan have gone through a process of attrition over the years so that only five or six companies compete in a sector which, in Europe, is occupied by twenty or more companies. EC companies still have to undergo the painful shrinkage process, and the dual threat of smarter European competition and leaner, fitter global competition could blow away the ill-prepared.

Moving into the detail of the strategy

A company's response to the single market will be affected by a number of factors:

- Proposed regulatory changes

- Current and future customers' requirements

- Competitor activity

- Supplier activity

- Market size and segmentation

Companies must bear in mind the level of potential benefits and the time that might be required to achieve them (Figure 14). Sometimes called the 'Three steps to success' approach, the model shows how the long-term goal of strategic innovation is based on earlier steps of efficiency and control within the organisation and the correct handling of enabling technologies.

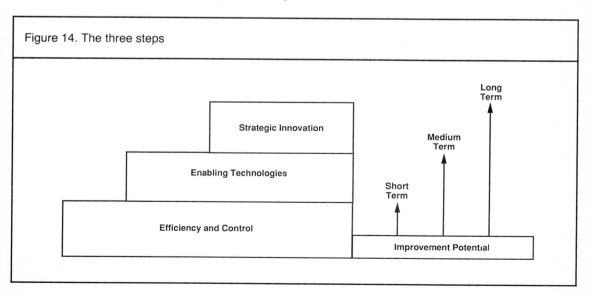

Figure 14. The three steps

Regulatory changes

Influencing legislation

Companies need to identify what legislation will affect them and in what form directives will be approved. There may still be a chance to influence the course of the legislation through trade bodies and representations. Companies must monitor the draft legislation for their sector if they are not to be adversely affected by changes. Those who lobby can sometimes influence the outcome. For example, UK tennis racket manufacturers discovered that EC legislation was going to make the Italian racket standard compulsory across the Community. Powerful lobbying by the UK was necessary to halt this.

Customer requirements

New entrants to the European market must discover what consumers buy, whether their choices are influenced by national restrictions that may soon change, and what their requirements are likely to be in a single market. The domestic UK consumer base should not be ignored as changes in taste and preference are likely to take place. Foreign competitors will be carrying out similar fact-finding exercises in the UK.

Competitor activity

Obtain information on competitors

A surprisingly large number of companies are wrong about who their continental competitors are. Their view of a competitor's capability and market tenacity is often clouded if the rival is a small subsidiary of a larger organisation. Basic data on competitors will have to be obtained to determine whether they have:

- Higher productivity
- Larger economies of scale
- Wider distribution networks
- A voice in setting technical standards
- Vertical/horizontal links with suppliers
- Links with larger organisations

Weaknesses may also be identified. Apart from being uncompetitive in any of the above, they may be inflexible, bureaucratic or lack the right type of personnel. Estimating the cost structure of a competitor is made easier if one element is considered at a time:

- Where are materials/components sourced?

- What is the number of employees, by category?

- Do they pay higher or lower salaries?

- What are their maximum and actual output levels?

- What type of manufacturing process do they use?

- How old is their plant and equipment?

Many competitors may already have a head start in Europe. Much can be learnt by seeing which of them are active and aggressive internationally and, if some of them have good strategies for 1992, it may be worth examining their strategies in detail before preparing your own.

Supplier capability

A pan-European purchasing policy may offer major cost savings if suppliers account for a major portion of a product's total cost. Shopping around may lead to hefty gains in price, quality, lead time and flexibility.

Market size and segmentation

Compete in the right segment

It will be important to select the right market size or segment in which to compete. Few businesses will be able to pursue every opportunity simultaneously and those that over-extend themselves will achieve little and expose themselves to possible takeover. Having laid the foundations of a new European strategy by looking at the competition, the next step is critical: it is essential to be ruthless in deciding what part of the company will provide the necessary resources for implementing the business strategy and, even more crucial, in ensuring that these resources are made available quickly.

It is important to know the precise definition of an industry. There are three factors determining any industry and, in practice, a business has all three elements:

- The basic needs that the products or services of a company are designed to meet

- The customers that buy these products and services

- The means of satisfying the customer's needs

A company that does not know its market can make fundamental mistakes: a US railway group believed it was simply in the (narrowly defined) rail business when in reality the company was operating in the travel business (a much broader definition of its industry). On the other hand, the Scandinavian airline SAS has clearly defined itself as being in the transport business, with an emphasis on caring for the customer, particularly the business traveller. Their concept of care stretches from the moment the business traveller leaves the front door of the home or office, to and from the airport, in the air, and in the hotel at the destination. SAS has expanded the concept of travel and has diversified into new areas but it has still remained within the strict definition of travel and customer care.

A company must, therefore, know its own size and market share compared with the rest of the industry and the share its competitors hold. It must be able to determine its overall profitability, know what resources are available to it and the rest of the industry, know its own strengths and weaknesses, and must have stated or implied strategies for coping with future competition.

The journey that companies will undertake to prepare for the changes triggered by 1992 will begin with the recognition of existing market conditions, but viewed through the filter of a well-defined, focused business strategy. The organisation's current position will evolve through consideration of corporate alternatives, followed by exploration and assessment, journeying through a phase of investigation and implementation, to a final evaluation which will allow the company's new market performance to be achieved and the impact assessed.

Aligning IT to the business strategy

To derive the maximum benefit from a business strategy, it should be aligned with the company's IT. There is no doubt that information systems have assumed a much greater corporate importance in many organisations in recent years. There is still however, a great deal of scepticism about the value that technology adds to business. This scepticism developed largely as the result of the failure of data-processing professionals to communicate their priorities and problems to those directing the business. Promising to deliver a great deal in a

Corporate scepticism

short time was a way of getting the necessary funds, but then cost and time over-runs brought many a data-processing department into disrepute. Problems were sometimes compounded when the jargon and technical niceties got in the way of communicating with business managers and end-users.

Although these days are largely over, many information systems units are still feeling their way towards their new role. This role places them firmly in support of the corporate business strategy, with systems there to support the critical business processes and to deliver services in a cost-effective manner. To achieve the correct position within the business strategy does, however, require extensive communications between those in charge of the business and those developing the information systems.

Many executives still need to be taught what information systems can do to improve their business. There are now so many areas of technological advance that keeping abreast of developments is a major task. The discussion between board and information systems cannot therefore take place within the context of the technology, other than in broad terms of the strategic options that are open to a company. Instead it must take place around the applications and business processes that can most benefit from technology support. Monitoring the benefits that have been realised from the earlier introduction of systems will permit fine tuning of the strategy and its implementation. This requires the active backing of the line managers who ultimately have to ensure the systems work in their business context, and who will want to monitor both the tangible and less tangible benefits from systems.

Monitor the benefits

Chief executives have a right to expect value for money from their IT investment, so the objectives of the business and the IT strategy preferred by the IT manager must match closely. If chief executives have their own business style and aspirations for the company, this must be understood by the IT community as well as by production and marketing directors. It is often the case that senior management uses one set of techniques or methodology for strategy planning, middle managers use different techniques for tactical planning and requirements definition, while IT staff use different techniques again for system development, and that at all levels the interfaces are inadequate. Thus techniques such as critical success factor analysis and value chain analysis are used by strategic planners, but the evaluation of technical options during IT feasibility studies is often based purely on hardware performance or ease of system maintenance. This must not be allowed to continue.

Ensure consistency

We have already considered the corporate value of information. Managing this information resource is a challenging task. Responsiblity for such management must lie within a single line. Split responsibilities will only cloud the issue. This means that all information resources – from library and research services, to computer systems, office systems, end-user computing, networks, telecommunications and management services – need to report to one director whose main concern is to exploit the information resource.

Formalise strategy

The information strategy will provide the foundation for the information technology strategy. This will evolve with the business. The potential business impact of the single market is so great that the IT strategy will need to be reviewed, and possibly revised. Although the strategy will evolve, this does not mean that the strategy can be informal. Many IT strategies have been informal in the past, but this will no longer be sufficient in an increasingly competitive business world. Strategy development is a catalyst for executive backing and corporate commitment to the information systems developments. It will lay the framework for individual projects and ensure that various developments will be capable of coming together into a coherent communications network within the company, and with other companies.

There are many things that the strategy needs to embrace, from the benefits that will be realised, to the resources needed to develop and support key user applications. The strategy will address the organisational issues, inside and outside the information systems department, and it will lay the framework for standards and policies which will determine supplier and third-party selection. The strategy exercise will also help to educate key executives and line managers to ensure they have a full and realistic appreciation of the financial and manpower resources needed to ensure the effective implementation of systems.

Developing the IT strategy

An IT strategy will apply information technology to all aspects of a business strategy, including:

- Warding off competitive threats
- Meeting corporate objectives
- Measuring and improving performance
- Keeping top management informed

There are obvious benefits which derive from compiling and implementing an effective IT strategy. These include:

- Investing in IT areas that contribute most to achieving corporate objectives

- Integrating business, technical and operational objectives

- Creating a corporate information system which meets the real needs of the business

However, it is not a static situation.

- The IT industry will change and hardware will continue to offer increased power at lower cost

- Technical trends are offering companies more open alternatives to the proprietary offerings from a single vendor

- Competitors, suppliers and customers will continue to look for and find better ways of doing business; and overall the business significance of IT will continue to increase

The company will also change. The typical boardroom should, therefore, abound with ideas and aspirations for using IT which need to be reconciled with limited resources, conflicting priorities and over-enthusiastic IT amateurs. If today's IT director is given corporate support and has an appropriate framework for formulating a business-led IT strategy, then the hurdles of previous eras can be forgotten, the credibility gap closed, and the true benefits of IT realised.

Sustaining competitive advantage

Robert Horne, one of Britain's largest independent paper merchants, developed a business strategy in the mid-1970s that was similar to that of many continental paper groups. It focused on centralised storage with a highly efficient computerised stock-control system. Its competitors initially doubted the wisdom of a single national warehouse feeding a network of local branches with overnight deliveries, but many have since imitated Horne.

For four to five years, the company had a clear advantage over its rivals and was able to improve its margins rather than lower prices by offering guaranteed twenty-four-hour delivery. The computerised warehouse was able to alert the buying department when certain stocks were low, while the sales department would be instructed to sell some lines or sizes of stocks that were not moving quickly enough. It allowed Horne to boost its stock turnover and monitor costly items still on the shelf.

Horne's achievement was evident, but it became diluted as more paper merchants adopted the strategy. By reversing its own policy of single storage location and building another, albeit smaller, warehouse in Scotland, it appeared that the company was admitting its orginal policy was flawed. However, advances in IT made it possible for this second unit to be integrated into the running of the company as if it were part of the main warehouse, although it was several hundred miles away. This strategy set out to enhance the quality of information to improve sales and the customer–supplier relationship. Like all of the best strategies it evolved to meet changing market circumstances.

Beyond competitive advantage

The advent of a barrier-free Europe obliges us to look beyond competitive advantage at the efficiency of organisations and how they will cope with information, technology and progress in the future. We must establish efficient, effective and responsive working environments fully supported by information technology. An effective information systems infrastructure can build barriers for competitors and establish firmer links with customers, while allowing the organisation to be flexible and responsive. The company can then seek a *series* of advantages rather than relying on a single advantage.

Determining priorities for 1992

At the higher levels business solutions will abound which are not technically feasible at the lower levels – often due to an outmoded and unadaptable technical infrastructure. This leads to frustration at the higher levels and, in many cases, people implementing solutions which are suitable for them alone, which merely adds to the chaos.

There will not be a uniformity of cost or benefit from the various activities that could be pursued. The challenge will be in meeting the opportunities that yield the greatest progress to the overall business goals. Careful selection of these will lead to success. A well focused IT strategy will effect major improvements in the running of the business through concentrating on the most beneficial applications. It is the set of business needs that should drive IT improvements.

The winners

As companies work out their strategy for 1992 (Figure 15), they will take account of a number of important factors which will determine their success or failure:

- The manufacturing location will influence the cost-effectiveness of the company. Decisions will have been made as to whether to manufacture in France or West Germany or to export from a single plant in the UK.

- Standardised products may reach a broader pan-European market despite the loss of some marginal sales.

- The product range will have been examined closely to see if the company can sustain a large number of products or whether it is better to concentrate resources on promoting a limited number of profitable products.

- The distribution network will have been rationalised and strengthened to link in more European countries.

- Information technology will underpin the company's entire business strategy for expansion in Europe.

The winners in a single market will have most or all of the following characteristics:

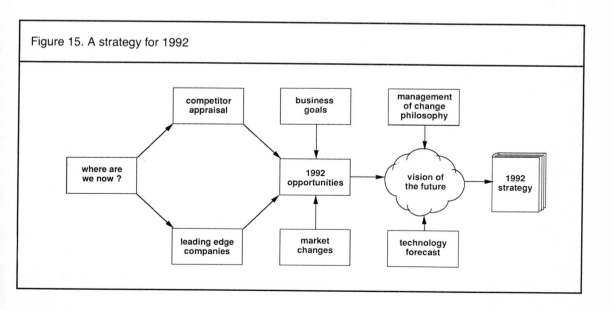

Figure 15. A strategy for 1992

- An obsession with quality in all parts of the company. Quality will mean satisfying customer needs first time every time and at minimum cost

- International personnel policies that emphasise training (not just in languages but also in management development) and secondment to enable personnel to become familiar with multiple cultures

- Unlimited flexibility

- A willingness to encourage managers to innovate and extract from the staff the maximum effort in a rapidly changing business environment

The degree of success of these 'winners' will be reflected in their ability to secure commitment from the base of the company's IT users and operators through middle management up to the board. All their efforts will be aimed at the customer through a dedication to the business strategy, and the planning and implementation that are needed to bring it to life. The 1992 strategy will be backed up by a hefty portfolio of corporate activity. This will have to cover everything from cultural changes to the speed and nature of implementation of new products, improved manufacturing procedures and pan-European marketing and sales.

II
The IT challenge

5.   Developing better products

Building a generation of Euro-products

We might expect a whole generation of Euro-products to develop, in an attempt to satisfy a dozen markets at once. However, if transnational products are to emerge, they will probably be global rather than solely European in their marketing. If a company goes to the trouble of establishing a pan-European product, it might as well try and enter the ranks of the few global brands that have made it to the top – Coca-Cola, Kellogg's Corn Flakes, Marlboro cigarettes and Levi jeans.

It is too early to talk about a typical European breakfast (despite the concept of continental breakfast) and it is unlikely that the French, Germans or Italians will be prepared to allow too much blurring of their traditional cuisines. The true European products will be those that can play a role on the global stage. Much development work has been done with the automobile, the single lens reflex camera, television and radio design and other electronic equipment so that they can be positioned in global markets and appeal to many diverse cultures. The same has yet to happen with clothes and food.

As pan-European products emerge, the advertising industry will need to broaden its horizons. Long association with a handful of multinational clients has enabled many advertising agencies to operate successfully in more than one market and culture at once. Most of the larger agencies have offices in all EC member states and are usually quite highly placed in terms of billings, compared with local operators. The advent of the single market will probably have only a limited impact on these agencies. The greater challenge lies ahead. European social conventions and demography are changing. Households will be smaller but more prosperous, more women will be in paid employment, and there will be more elderly people but fewer teenagers.

Business and finance are areas where pan-European products will probably emerge first. The UK may be able to build on its dominant position as a financial centre and other sectors may enjoy the benefits of such dominance. Now is not the time to be complacent, however. The early indications are that the French smart card, an ordinary plastic credit card with a microprocessor and memory chip built in, will open up whole new markets and products. Based on technology developed in the 1970s, there are now over 17 million smart cards in France. Two pilot schemes by Barclays and Midland are under way in the UK. Is there a danger of losing our finance sector advantage because of the impact of a new technology?

R&D assumes a new importance

Technological breakthroughs will change the course of some industries. For example, the commercialisation of genetic engineering has seen the establishment of hundreds of new research-dominated companies that are bringing new pharmaceutical and agricultural products to the market.

The demands of making products in changing circumstances provide the focus for examining functions in companies. All manufacturing-based companies and most large service businesses need some element of R&D to gain or hold on to their technological lead, or simply to keep pace with the competition (Figure 16). One of the basic problems with R&D has been that it has frequently been seen as an act of faith in the company's future.

R&D a strategic resource

R&D has to be recognised as a strategic resource. Management needs to know the implications of the R&D that it is investing in. It also needs to feel itself in control of the innovation process, to know that the research being undertaken will provide value for money by enhancing the company's competitive position and it will need to ask

---

Figure 16. Issues for R&D

o Need for genuine innovation

o Time to market

o Market penetration during patent life

o Shortage of human resources

o Increasing regulatory requirements

o Need for products to be international

o Cost

---

itself three questions: Can we make it? Is there a market for it? Are the margins right? This applies pressure on the R&D director or the chief technology officer to justify the allocation of scarce resources to meet the strategic aims of the company. The R&D director suddenly needs to be able to talk to other senior managers in their language and deal with the business implications and marketing potential of the hoped-for technological gains. At the same time senior managers must be educated to build in a technological dimension to their own strategic planning, and to recognise the difficulties of product development as a result of 1992 (Figure 17).

Figure 17. Product development difficulties after 1992

o **New markets**

o **Shorter product life-cycles**

o **Differentiation of products**

o **Unpredictable economic and technological changes**

o **Many products in last phase of life-cycle**

o **Need new manufacturing technology to increase quality and reduce costs**

o **Increasing productivity leading to over-capacity**

o **Growth in the areas of biotechnology, chemicals and plastics, and environmental technology**

Cut development time

Estimates of how long it will take to bring a concept to the market are hopelessly unreliable. A recent survey in the USA showed that the lead time for commercial production of an idea varied from three to twenty-five years. Many companies, however, operate in an environment that is transfixed by quarterly or interim profit statements and which does not put much value on quality innovations that may take a decade to yield results. By cutting the development time, companies can have the best of both worlds. Ford has trimmed vital months off parts of its pre-production design while Rank Xerox has developed a photocopier in three years instead of the five years it took for a comparable earlier product.

This acceleration emphasises development rather than research. Management can thus ruthlessly weed out unprofitable projects at an early stage by examining the development requirements in parallel with the research activity. It can also spend more earlier in the hope of gaining working products and it can determine that a project's development is 'good enough' for the market.

An 'ideal' product may fail in the market because a less-than-ideal product managed to get established there first. On the other hand, products that fail in the R&D phase need not be consigned to the dustbin. 3M, the US office products company, developed a new adhesive that failed every conventional definition of sticking paper together. In fact, the adhesive would not bind anything together at all. The product's failings were turned into attributes and the company produced the 'Post-it' notepads that can be stuck securely but impermanently on any piece of office equipment, paper or furniture.

Rejuvenating existing products

Not everyone will be able to produce new products in time for 1992, so existing product ranges, in some cases supported by stalwarts several decades old, may have to act as a stop-gap. It will be possible to rejuvenate existing products and offer them to markets that were not open to them before. There will be some additional expense in this, but not necessarily a doubling or trebling of marketing effort. Despite classic rules of economic theory, the market is not a uniform landscape. There are areas where more effort is required than others and where some products will flourish and others will wither and die. The US brewer Anheuser Busch discovered, for example, that while a 50 per cent increase in its advertising budget increased sales by 7 per cent, a 25 per cent decrease in the same budget, in comparable regions, led to a sales increase of 14 per cent. The lesson is that

Experiment

experimentation is important and that it is easy to make incorrect assumptions about the relationship between advertising and sales.

Trying to breathe new life into tired old products can be more difficult than simply trying to find new markets for them, however, the same product in a different country is often so different in terms of its competitive advantage that it might as well be a new product. The competition in the new market is as different as are the consumers' expectations and their awareness of the product's qualities. Coca-Cola, although a global brand, has substantially different patterns of use in different countries. Ovaltine is synonymous with putting the British to sleep, yet French consumers expect to be able to send their children off to school with its warming effects in their tummies. In Nigeria, it is linked with couples going off to bed and enjoying good sex. The possibilities, it would appear, are endless.

Product quality

Rejuvenating old products can strengthen the competitive position of companies, but there is an extra factor that must be considered: product quality. The new trading conditions in the EC may make it easier to fall foul of regulations on product quality. Older products, if they have not been designed with quality and automated assembly in mind, may be more at risk than new innovations. Unless manufacturers are prepared to scrutinise their product's fitness for use in the broadest sense, they will be faced with stiff competition, from within Europe and overseas.

Building in quality

Much of the post-war success of the Japanese economy has been attributed to the relentless pursuit of quality in their products. Dr W. Edwards Deming, a US statistician, told leading Japanese industrialists in the early 1950s that by concentrating on quality, they could take on and beat US companies by supplying reliable goods at lower prices. 'I told the Japanese that they would capture world markets in five years,' says Dr Deming.

In some cases it has taken a little longer, but the result is still the same:

- *Watches*: Between 1976 and 1985, Japanese watchmakers (Seiko, Casio and Citizen) increased their share of the UK watch market from 9 per cent to 29 per cent, while the market grew by more than 50 per cent.

- *Videos*: JVC, Hitachi, Sony, Panasonic and Sanyo seized and held 74 per cent of the UK video market over ten years.

- *Camera film*: As the UK market doubled in size during the 1980s, Fuji's market share soared from 2 per cent to 12 per cent.

- *Automobiles*: Japanese carmakers held a UK market share of 0.5 per cent in 1970 and developed it into its current 11 per cent.

- *Motorcycles*: From holding a one-third share of the UK market in 1970, Japanese motorcycle manufacturers control over 90 per cent today.

Although quality may appear to cost the manufacturer initially, the consumer is quite prepared to pay higher prices if guarantees of quality exist. A recent Gallup poll in the US found that members of the public were prepared to pay 135 per cent more for a pair of shoes, 74 per cent more for a couch, 66 per cent more for a television set, 55 per cent more for a dishwasher, and 36 per cent more for a car, if they perceived it to be a quality product.

Quality will mean different things in different products. A Rolls-Royce is a quality car by any definition. But so is a Ford Fiesta. Both meet the quality standards for their particular category of product and are perceived to be quality goods.

Shortening product lives bring dangers and opportunities

As a general rule, modern products have life-cycles that have been shortened by competitive pressure. A company must be able to show new developments to existing products or brands in a bid to reassure consumers that the product is the best that money can buy. Competitors will claim a 'new, improved' dimension to rival products in order to woo customers, even though the only change to the product might be subtle alterations to packaging and presentation. Pressure is then placed on the other manufacturer to produce not only a similar improvement but one that exceeds the original improvement.

Pressure will also exist for the introduction of entirely new products. This pressure will normally come from within a manufacturing company rather than from the consuming public. If public demand drove product development there would be higher success rates for new product launches. But if the market research has been lucky enough to identify an untapped market or the chance to develop a new one, the rewards for the company that launches a successful new consumer brand are enormous.

Traditional approaches to R&D, from technician and management alike, will need to change if new market opportunities are to be exploited. Some of the available information technology aids like desk-top manufacturing of prototypes, research databases, computer conferencing, and expert systems must be used to produce a more cost effective and focused R&D effort.

Product transferability

The immediacy of the single market has posed a dilemma for all EC manufacturers. Will existing product ranges sell in other member states once legal, fiscal and distribution barriers have been removed, or must companies redesign, remake and repackage existing products? Consumer goods manufacturers will be tempted to standardise products – and their advertising – to achieve economies of scale, but many will find that new product development will need to be tailored to individual markets. This will mean shorter and more varied product life-cycles.

Dangers of shorter life-cycles

The emphasis on shorter life-cycles may make most existing product lines redundant within just a few years. A danger zone exists when the shortening product life equals or is less than the time it takes to bring new products to market. The consequence of this will be that a company has old products on sale and will lose share in the market place to companies with fuller product ranges. US computer group Hewlett-Packard, for instance, derives 80 per cent of its turnover from products that have been launched within the past three years.

Companies that position themselves with flexible design and manufacturing strategies that are based on short production runs for different markets will have a commanding strategic advantage. It may not be necessary to produce twelve different types of toothpaste for the EC market, but it might be necessary to market three or four in different ways. For a company that knows how to make and market toothpaste in only one way (and refuses to change) this will be a major problem.

Product design

By shortening the product design cycle, competitive advantage can be gained. This is one of the most important aspects in the fight for European market share. In simple terms, the key to leading the market will be the ability to choose the right product and then to bring this to market rapidly and profitably. This will require teams of product designers and production engineers working much more closely together during the early evolution of the product idea (Figure 18). To achieve this it is important to understand the customers' requirements so that the product design actually meets these needs.

Product definition systems

Products must be developed over the shortest possible time. This requires systems that help in product definition so that customer requirements are understood and the product is specified to match these needs. A knowledge of the state of various technologies is important so that full advantage is taken of new developments. Once the product has been defined, design of the product and its manufacturing process must be undertaken.

The methodology for product design is well advanced and uses many techniques from the car manufacturing industry. These techniques and others help to define the 'right' product, and ensure that all aspects of its design have been considered by all the relevant people within the business. The use of these systems will help to ensure that all design aspects are well defined and understood early in the design

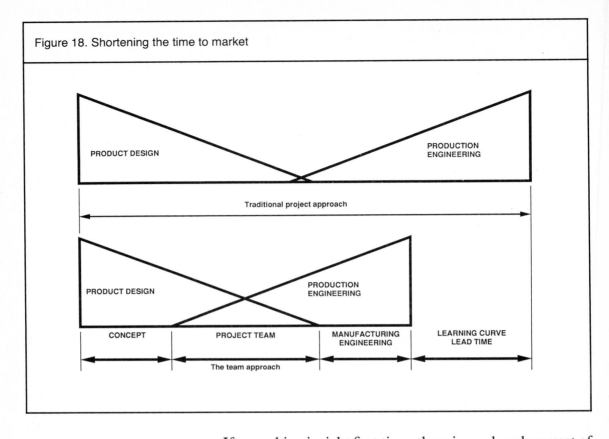

Figure 18. Shortening the time to market

PRODUCT DESIGN

PRODUCTION ENGINEERING

Traditional project approach

PRODUCT DESIGN

PRODUCTION ENGINEERING

CONCEPT | PROJECT TEAM | MANUFACTURING ENGINEERING | LEARNING CURVE LEAD TIME

The team approach

process. If everything is right first time, there is a reduced amount of redesign and very little needs to be 'put right' at the manufacturing stage. By using such methods, the product definition and design stages will take longer, but there will be little or no need for redesign. Costs will be cut, as it is cheaper to erase a line on pieces of paper or on a computer screen than it is to redesign and manufacture a new piece of process equipment.

Computer-aided design

Flexible manufacturing cells offer organisations more control over the individual parts of the design and manufacturing process. Computer-aided design is one aspect of this trend and it embraces fully integrated manufacture, assembly and packaging. Shop-floor production equipment, for example, can be tailored to producing short runs of trial goods for test marketing before large capital investment is made.

Companies that hope to achieve a radical shortening of the design cycle will need to think of themselves as an integrated system, a linked chain of internal customers and suppliers that continually delivers high quality and value to the company's internal and external customers. People need to know their individual or group roles in an organisation and how their activities relate to and affect others within the business. They need to know how the work, information and data flow within the organisation and the importance of minimising the overall time cycle. They need to know that it is important to be right first time so that there is no need to spend time and money putting things right later. As people become aware of the contribution they can make to the product development process they will be able to identify where further time may be saved. IT will help to analyse and improve the process.

Small multi-functional teams can help shorten the design process by ensuring that people communicate all the time and that all relevant aspects of the design are considered early in the design process. Rapid feedback 'loops' can be built in to ensure that potential problems are trapped early. One of the real challenges in winning new European markets will be in maximising the use of corporate knowledge in the different value-added phases. There has been a changing relationship between the traditional components of business activity over the past two decades. Whereas the amount of capital that a company uses in any product or service has remained proportionally the same over the last twenty years, the element of corporate know-how has increased dramatically, usually at the expense of the labour and overhead elements. Although management expertise has been directed towards cutting labour and overhead costs in this period, the potential benefits of pursuing this type of management activity in the future are limited. Greater gains are to be made by directing managerial efforts into locating, developing and supplying new markets with new products in increasingly shorter periods of time.

Product design and automation

Getting the most from automation

One of the growing tasks of the design function in modern manufacturing is to help senior management ensure the company gets the most out of its automation. Gains can sometimes be achieved by simple redesigning and the cost savings through design changes must not be confused with the improvements from automation. Nevertheless, there are undoubtedly major benefits to be gained from designing for automated manufacture in many situations.

Simplification

The key to designing products that can be automated is to simplify the product as much as possible. When components of complex products do not lend themselves to simplification, automation may prove too difficult or too costly. The solution may then be a mechanically assisted assembly that is fully integrated into a manual assembly line.

Of crucial importance to understanding the role and effectiveness of design in automation is the fact that simplifying industrial components does not necessarily reduce their costs. Components often need to be of a higher quality than those used for manual assembly and need to be made to finer tolerances. Automation needs to be flexible if it is to respond to changing product design and production volumes. The use of individual anthropomorphic robots can provide flexibility and production growth in small steps. With average costs between £20,000 and £25,000, an array of robots spreads the risk of plant failure and can permit substantial modification in future product designs. The entire array can be geared for one sort of production, or individual robots may be dedicated to products for say France and West Germany and others for the rest of Europe. By standardising the make of a robot, maintenance and spare parts can be kept to a minimum. Training programmes can also be designed for Europe as a whole instead of individual countries.

Product designers need to be involved in the development of overall corporate strategies because if a design is not what a market wants or is too expensive to make, a company's entire strategy is at risk. Designers must not only simplify the products they create, but must also simplify the entire design process.

Building new products

Different industries have different development cycles. Development is not one activity but many. The techniques that are applied during the design phase of a new product are radically different from those needed for the production engineering of the project.

To examine the critical elements of a successful product requires a development cycle model that charts the progress of an idea through to its launch into the market place and beyond. The major phases of this model are:

- Product idea
- Feasibility study
- Laboratory model
- Development
- Production engineering
- Production

- Trials

- Launch

- Sales and support

For successful product development the whole process must be managed well and tested against market reaction at every stage. As a company faces increasing competition from the single market, it should ensure not just that these individual functions are performed well but also that there is effective information exchange between the different elements. Competitive advantage will come from the whole process's being tightly integrated, not from excellence in one or more stages.

Product idea

The original idea for a product can come from anywhere and every company has a different attitude to new ideas. Some organisations smother ideas at birth, while others take them seriously only if they come from certain parts of the company. Although it may be costly in the short term, the most productive approach is to consider all ideas, regardless of origin, on their commercial and technical merits. For example, Toyota received 1.7 million suggestions from its workforce in 1984 on ways to improve its operations and implemented 96 per cent of them. On the other hand, virtually the entire senior management of Sony was against the concept of the Walkman portable cassette player. The one exception and sole champion of the idea was the company's chairman who persisted in the face of corporate opposition and transformed an entire electronics industry as a result.

Feasibility study

These studies are best carried out by a small team of two or three to assess the market and address key technical issues before any large commitments are made. The main issues are:

- Is it possible to make it? Do you have the right technology or must it be bought or imported? If so, will it be possible to get it up and running before 1992?

- How much will it cost? External sourcing of components can give the manufacturing organisation greater flexibility. As greater sourcing of material takes place, raw material costs will be less subject to a range of variables such as local demand in the source country, relative inflation rates and currency fluctuations. Keeping the cost of production, and therefore the sales cost, down should mean greater demand.

- How long will it take? The range of materials and technologies available might mean that manufacturers are spoilt for choice. It is important to know what is necessary, find it and buy it.

- What skills will be needed? New product development may mean importing skills from other companies or countries. If insufficient skills exist in an organisation, they must be acquired rapidly before demand either pushes up their price or limits their availability.

- What is the market? The rapidly changing EC environment will mean that there are many fundamental changes to existing markets and assumptions over how markets are to be defined.

- How big is it? The total market is 320 million people. If business strategies and product development are geared for global markets instead of simply European markets, this total will be easily doubled. On the other hand, within Europe there will be many small market niches that may be ignored by larger companies initially.

- When is it? The real market forces that will determine the shape of Europe in the next decade are already at work and the future of some individual markets (such as electronics) will be determined more rapidly than others.

- What price will it stand? Organisations will need to determine what price resistance levels for their products exist in other member states. A £10 barrier on a product price may exist in the UK but precise currency conversions such as Fr 110, DM 32.50, L23,850 or BFr 685 are unlikely to bear any relation to actual price barriers on the same product in these other markets.

- What features does it require? More sophisticated consumer markets will demand more product features and accessories. Similarly these markets will be more demanding of the after-sales service function.

- How receptive is the market to changes in price, features or timing? This will vary according to country and the level of competition within industries.

- What development cash flow is needed? Tough decisions need to be taken on other products/projects if the necessary cash flow is to be generated. There may be a case for running down one product and diverting all the profits from it to a 1992 hopeful.

- What is the necessary capital outlay? The highly developed capital markets in the City of London could give UK companies a substantial lead over Continental competitors, but the City connection must be educated, developed and encouraged. Finance organisations must view investment in product design infrastructure as a long-term investment.

- What is the return on investment? Medium- to long-term investment strategies are necessary. There will be very few short-term gains and one- to three-year investment timescales should be avoided.

- What is the payback period? There will not be any immediate returns and because Europe will remain a highly competitive arena any immediate profits may need to be re-invested. Success could be measured by the time it takes for a product to break even, taking into account all R&D, production and product launch expenditure. This may help to distinguish between competing priorities.

- How sensitive is the product to volume fluctuations? This will vary depending on market developments, level of competition and consumer demands.

All these issues will need to be addressed in some detail before the company commits large-scale investment to any new product idea for the European market.

Laboratory model

This is the first step in producing a working example of the product or system. It is physical proof that the concept works although it may bear little resemblance to the final product. Its importance increases, however, if the product is using new technologies because both risk and cost are kept to a minimum at this point. It is also vital to ensure that broad and multi-disciplinary capability is injected into the product's planning and development. Often advances come from the application of knowledge in one area to a new area.

Development

This is the heart of the project and where most of the money is spent. The important questions are: How?, How much? and How long? The project team should be assembled progressively with attention to both their skills and their personalities.

The team will need to look at system design, module design, implementation, integration and testing.

Production engineering

The development phase proves that the product can be made once. The next stage in product development is normally production engineering which must show that the product can be made hundreds or thousands of times. This phase of the project will tackle many of the following:

- Cost of manufacture
- Cost of components
- Cost of assembly
- Test procedures and equipment
- Manufacturing documentation
- Component procurement
- Environmental effects
- Robustness
- Reliability
- Safety
- Regulations
- Packaging

The multiplicity of markets will now offer manufacturing companies a wide choice of manufacturing and assembly locations. The cost structures of each location will need to be determined and strategic decisions on proximity to the market or to a distribution network will have to be taken. Manufacturing costs in different locations will vary, so continual attention to the relative benefits of each possibility will be necessary.

Sourcing

Even if a manufacturing operation is established in one country, the sourcing of materials and components need not come from the same country. As distribution costs fall and transport links between the member states grow, the choice of suppliers will increase. Small changes in the design of products may also permit cheaper sourcing of alternative components not normally available to UK manufacturers. Partial or sub-assembly may become an option, with final assembly taking place within each market. This will enable companies to differentiate their products further. Although this may appear to lengthen the supply chain, it may be necessary to use such techniques in order to compete in certain markets. IT will support such developments.

Testing

Testing of new products and processes will need to be taken a step further than in the domestic market. The move towards common standards will gain pace the closer we get to 1992, but in the meantime British products will need to be tested to standards applicable elsewhere.

Similarly the product or service will need to meet more stringent consumer demands. Expectations of reliability vary not only from country to country but within regions of each country. Perceptions of safety also differ and the product engineering phase must address the simultaneous satisfaction of numerous safety standards.

Packaging

The need for multi-lingual packaging will affect either the design phase (placing product details in every language on the same package) or the assembly phase (where different packaging is used for each country). Quality of documentation will also be an important differentiator.

More than any other phase, production engineering in the multi-national environment needs a methodical approach and total attention to detail.

Production

The product's manufacturing process is handed over to the factory.

Trials

Field trials often identify glaring errors missed by the development team simply because no one thought the product would be used in a particular manner. This is the last chance to avoid embarrassing mistakes. The room for generating mistakes and not catching them in time will increase dramatically as companies gear up to service a large number of markets simultaneously.

Launch

A launch of new products or services may be progressive, with trial regions or countries used as test-beds. A company which feels confident that it has tended to every production and marketing detail may, however, opt to go for the 'Big Bang' approach with a simultaneous launch in each market. The rewards, as well as the risks, of this approach can be significant.

Sales and support

New standards of product accounting may be necessary in the single market. Simple manufacturing costs may no longer provide a reliable guide to the actual cost the company has incurred in putting a product into the market place. Marketing costs will become more important as a multiplicity of consumers are targeted with the same or similar goods. Selling costs will be higher. The sales network will be larger because the market will be bigger. Agencies or dealerships will bypass some of the start-up costs in new markets, but the operational costs of the infrastructure will still be there. Support and service costs will gradually increase in significance in the product's profit/loss account, as will the element of financing that will be needed to entice new customers to buy the products.

The need to stay flexible

As the UK moves towards 1992, it will become clearer how far consumers are prepared to alter existing buying patterns. But at the moment it is uncertain whether nationalistic feelings alone will persuade consumers to buy local goods or whether other determining factors such as product quality, value for money and convenience will dominate. The hope is that local markets will accept products on their inherent qualities rather than on the basis of their country of origin.

What is certain, however, is that manufacturing industry will need to achieve greater flexibility in output. The new markets are only one of the factors to be considered in the single market. Global competition and collaboration through mergers and acquisition will accelerate while product life-cycles will change and product differentiation will become more important. There will be a greater exchange of data and information while companies try to gain competitive advantage over their rivals. Most unsettling will be the unpredictability of economic and technological changes that will transform markets and the perception of market potential.

To produce for global consumption, companies will have to use Europe as a base for the initial economies of scale, but the European production capability will itself need to be flexible. It will be possible to achieve much of this in the manufacturing process but elements of it will need to be designed directly into the product and into the design processes that bring new products to market. IT will play an important role in guaranteeing this flexibility.

At the end of the day, the original manufacturing costs will represent only a very small part of the total cost of a product. A company's exposure to rampant cost escalation down the line will be determined by its attitude towards, and success in implementing, the principles of total quality management.

The additional factors of time, distance, culture, language and currency exchange rates will magnify the scale of manufacturing mistakes. It is one thing despatching a replacement component up the M1 to a disgruntled customer, and it is something else trying to get that same component to a dissatisfied client in Milan on the same day! Quality of product design is the key, as is the responsiveness of the product design process. These two factors of quality and responsiveness are also important in manufacturing, as we shall see.

6. The factory of the future today

Competitive advantage and the value chain

One of the most crucial factors in guaranteeing the future of a business organisation is its competitive advantage over its competitors. Michael Porter argues that competitive advantage cannot be understood by looking at a firm as a whole. Instead it is necessary to realise that a company is 'a collection of activities that are performed to design, produce, market, deliver and support its product'.

The most visible portion of this value chain must be the factory – whether it is a nuclear power station generating electricity for the national grid, or a Jaguar assembly plant producing cars for export. It is one of the few areas in which management can see at first hand the impact of decisions that have already been taken in the R&D and design stages. It is also one of the most scrutinised areas of industrial activity simply because it is easy to see the impact of an innovation on production line output.

Information's role in distribution and manufacturing

It is likely that flexible manufacturing systems will be needed to shorten production runs after 1992 and that advanced manufacturing techniques will offer a low cost route to such flexibility. But this is only a beginning. A flexible factory can be made even more productive when it is integrated with other parts of the company. Distribution channels for example will be equally important in determining the overall profitability of the company.

Integrating all functions
It is through IT that companies can define, gather, store, manipulate, and communicate data to smooth the flow of information. The computer, and the IT associated with the computer, is the tool that allows integration of a wide spectrum of manufacturing and distribution activities (Figure 19).

78

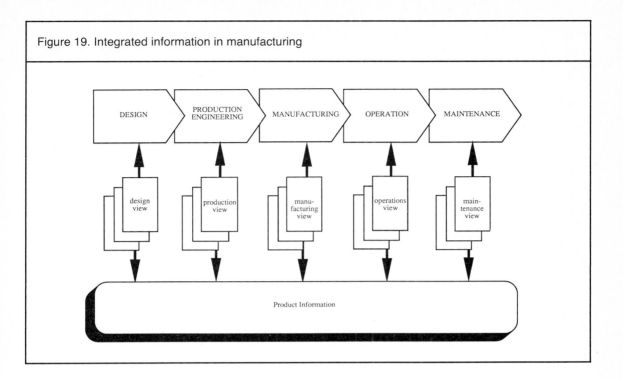

Figure 19. Integrated information in manufacturing

It is important to be aware of the changes taking place in the engineering control function as companies move towards integrated manufacturing and distribution. Years ago engineering control only applied to the drawing or print of a component. Today we must not only control the electronic representation of the part – the print being only a physical manifestation – but we must also control the associated process software that is involved with the manufacture of the product itself. This could be everything from the routing or process plan to the software used to drive the robot, the vision systems, the co-ordinate measuring machine or a host of other electronically controlled devices on the manufacturing floor.

In the future the links between customer behaviour and production will be much enhanced, and as a result distribution will form an integral part of the value chain, and will enable the smart organisation to offer even higher levels of customer service.

Companies need a flexible response because of the heightened expectations of industrial customers and lay consumers. In essence, the manufacturer that can offer significantly faster delivery has a major competitive advantage. Rapid delivery can be achieved by massive stock levels which invariably lead to writing off obsolete goods and adding to total product costs, or it can be gained by making

**Customer
expectations rising**

goods only when a customer wants them. The difference is a matter of 'just in time' rather than 'just in case'.

Whether a customer is a prime contractor or an end-user, the customer's expectations can rise very quickly because of what is seen to be happening elsewhere in the world. Customers are demanding major improvements in quality, service and price, at regular intervals. One major European car manufacturer has given suppliers contracts which decrease 1.5 per cent in value each year because they are expected to drive down costs continually. The price of a colour television illustrates the gains that can be achieved for both the consumer and the manufacturer: twenty years ago a colour television cost ten weeks' average pay, compared to one and a half weeks' pay today. As demand for choice and functionality increases, the number of possible product variations soars and products become more complex. A Japanese electronics manufacturer introduces over 1,000 new products each year, while there are up to 2 billion theoretical variants of some European car models.

Planning and control on a European scale

Multinationals have wrestled with the problem of manufacturing and distribution systems in more than one country for many years. Large organisations have typically supplied many distribution points throughout Europe (and beyond) from one or more manufacturing sites, each in turn quite possibly supplied from vendors in several countries.

Currency fluctuations, different cost developments, language/communications problems and international configuration/quality control have challenged management teams for many years. As the single market becomes more of a reality, an increasing number of companies need to deal with these problems. The future belongs to those who take advantage of a large market place as true pan-European players, using their full corporate resources to develop, produce and market their products as internationally recognised leaders. Some will be able to simplify their logistics chain by supplying individual countries from a plant or plants dedicated to more than one country. They may split Europe into trading areas, whereas others, by virtue of economies of scale or small volumes of specific products within a broad product range, will not be able to do so. It is apparent that an increasing number of manufacturing companies will need to develop strategies and tactical plans to enable them to deal with multinational sourcing, manufacture and distribution in increasingly complex patterns.

The multinational issues

Multinational supply-chain management has tended to organise plants to support a local region with the general justifications of:

- Supporting local markets
- Marketing benefit of local manufacture
- Reduced transport and distribution costs
- Supply security from multi-plant manufacture of a specific product
- Less product cost uncertainty from currency fluctuations

Purchasing traditionally concentrated on local suppliers, so that the multinational problem was minimised. In future, more complex supply chains and multinational manufacturing facilities will become more common as companies aim to supply multinational distribution centres or end customers from specially focused factories.

Multi-country sourcing

The reduction of border delays, administrative problems and tax- and bureaucracy-related costs will make multinational sourcing more attractive. While the alignment of different quality or performance standards is likely to take a long time, purchasing staff need to remain conscious of such differences. This calls for increased specification of international standards and a much closer relationship with suppliers. It is important not only for the seller to become eloquent in many languages and conscious of local laws, customs and habits, but the buyer, too, needs to build up such skills to ensure that he can appreciate and manage the many culture-related problems which are likely to arise.

Multinational sourcing, particularly that which involves long-term vendor–customer relationships, will continue to suffer from currency fluctuations. This is probably the greatest single inhibitor of confident, long-term, international logistics management. The European Monetary System (EMS) should reduce the unpredictability of fluctuations for those member states who participate.

The complex logistics chain

As the logistics chain becomes more complex, its management must become more sophisticated. One would expect a small central logistics group to manage the overall supply–demand interface and deal specifically with the moderation and normalisation of forecasts, and the long-term strategic issues of balancing anticipated future demand with building up supply capacity. It is unlikely that central planners will be able to manage the daily capacity control of individual plants in an effective manner.

In the past, tactical plant loading and detailed, central balancing of supply and demand across multiple factories was common among the larger multinationals. Their factories used to have duplication in capacity, allowing central planners to manage such daily loading. Most companies found this difficult to manage, and it is unlikely to be a key feature in future multinational supply–demand management.

There has also been process specialisation, so that specific factories have specialised in specific technologies and have provided a European-wide (or even worldwide) service. Specialist component manufacturers supporting assembly plants (e.g. in the automotive industry) are and will be popular, with feeder plants increasingly treated as external vendors in a supply chain. On the other hand, a situation where two plants assemble the same product but each supplies the other with common components is likely to be discouraged to reduce traditional problems of configuration control and interchangeability. Equally, plants exchanging components and sub-assemblies in a complex two-directional logistics flow pattern is likely to be less popular. Manageability has shown itself to be complex and difficult in such situations.

Distribution management

Once we accept the concept of focused factories, each specialising on a narrowing range of complete products, then the co-ordination of distribution becomes significant. Where each product is sold as an individual unit (e.g. domestic appliances), the problem is relatively small, but where multiple products from a number of factories need to be configured into complex systems, such co-ordination can be extremely difficult.

It is quite common for distribution centres to take the role of the co-ordinator and establish a normal customer–supplier relationship with their supplying manufacturing plants. For example, a supplier of complex electronic systems arranges all sub-units within one system to be delivered to one of its plants, where the system is assembled and tested prior to being disassembled and crated for shipment to the installation site.

To ensure good customer delivery performance within low stock buffers, it is necessary to develop an excellent delivery date achievement within the constraints of 'guaranteed' performance to specification and flawless management of delivery of units shipped from different factories. If that is not achieved, distribution and installation management is likely to be ineffective, frustrating and expensive. Central configuration support, logistics co-ordination and quality assurance are likely to be significant features in complex multinational supply-chain management.

Distribution skills will play a key role

In its simplest form, distribution is the warehousing, handling and transport of goods. It has been argued that distribution encompasses all processes that do not change the basic form of the product – this would embrace stock management, purchasing and supply management, sales and marketing. The distribution function will grow in significance in the single market. Cross-border trade within the EC in 1988 amounted to over $360 billion.

West Germany is the largest exporter of goods within the EC, exporting over a quarter of the total internal exports. But West Germany is also a major importer from other member states and has only a small $4 billion internal trade surplus. The UK lies fourth (after the Netherlands' $55 billion and France's $52 billion) with exports to other member states worth $47 billion. The league table for imports from other member states is little different:

West Germany	$90 billion
France	$65 billion
UK	$51 billion
Benelux	$40 billion
Netherlands	$38 billion

UK distribution represents 13 per cent of gross domestic product (GDP) and employs 20 per cent of the UK labour force. However, it receives substantially less investment than manufacturing industry although its contribution to the economy is roughly the same. With the advent of the single market, distribution is bound to assume a greater importance in many companies.

Distribution will change radically in the single market. In the past, cross-border goods flows from the UK into Europe have been relatively large shipments, but as these movements become easier and cheaper, the distribution depot network in Europe will have to be rationalised. Many more shipments will be delivered directly to the customer, and this will increase the importance of the storage and handling of goods within companies.

Direct control of distribution

By taking control of part of the distribution function, companies can enhance their potential profitability or gain a substantial competitive edge. Sainsbury's seized control of its supply chain with the result that the stocks, warehousing and transport for 80 per cent of its sales are now controlled by the company. Most suppliers deliver direct to Sainsbury's regional warehouses, which manage the stock and transport to individual retail outlets in their area.

On the face of it, this adds an extra link in the supply chain. In reality it concentrates stock in limited areas, allows more selling space in the supermarkets, and reduces handling time at each store because a fleet of lorries from different manufacturers is replaced by Sainsbury's own relatively small number of vehicles. Sainsbury's also manages to achieve, through IT, an overview of the company's total requirements. For all companies involved in distribution a higher use of IT in warehousing will be needed to overcome language difficulties on labelling, achieve a tracking of goods within the warehouse, select a destination for the goods and allow stock rotation and shelf-life monitoring.

Manufacturing – the recent past

Manufacturing has had a poor image in the UK over the past thirty years. Our US, Japanese and European competitors have displayed remarkable skills at producing the right goods for the right price, while the UK has been content to trade on its name as a world-class manufacturer. Great strides, however, have been made in the past ten years and some of the productivity gap that existed between the UK and her main industrial competitors has been narrowed.

UK engineering scored repeated successes in developing North Sea oil and gas fields in the 1970s, while the financial services industry held people in awe with its roller coaster ride from Big Bang in 1986 to the

October crash in 1987. In contrast, factories or production have displayed, as a rule, little glamour or sense of adventure. This has made it difficult to recruit quality people.

Need for quality personnel

The lack of a steady stream of quality graduates into UK manufacturing has taken its toll. Those keen on manufacturing careers and mobile enough to travel have beaten paths to the doors of US and European competitors, and provided them with the benefit of a highly trained generation of managers and technicians who possessed important insights into UK markets. Engineers in the UK have been under-represented at the highest levels within companies, in stark contrast to other countries, particularly West Germany. Accounting, not production or marketing, has been the driving force in too many UK companies.

A healthy manufacturing base is an essential ingredient for any country that hopes to enjoy a leading position in European and world markets after 1992. The quality and efficiency of UK manufacturing will be the litmus test for our success or failure. Several important aspects of manufacturing were undergoing rapid change even before the decision to pursue a single market was taken.

Manufacturing has always sought cheap labour but the scale of demand has now changed. Instead of seeking cheap labour on a national or continental scale, companies have extended the search to a global basis. This happens already in the car and electronics industries with plants set up by US and Japanese companies in Wales, Scotland, Spain, Portugal, Ireland and, increasingly, Greece. When the labour force is also required to be well trained (often to university level), stable and highly motivated, companies need to examine all possible locations. The task of finding enough bright, cheap workers close to a major market is becoming increasingly difficult.

Current trends in manufacturing

The greatest market share increasingly belongs to the large industrial players who have the resources and sophistication to invest continuously in research and development, and who have the marketing 'muscle' to penetrate their market sector aggressively. The challenge they face is the ability to generate rapid response, short product introduction times, low overheads, low inventories, high product variety – all the normal characteristics of smaller companies. The call is for smaller, more specialised focused factories. Single Policy Unit (SPU) is a term coined for a manufacturing unit that consists of a logical grouping of resources, that strongly aligns with the competitive

Focused factories

needs of the business and that simplifies the management and logistics of the total operation.

The increasing product range and variety demanded by customers means an increasing number of SPUs, supporting jointly a co-ordinated sales and marketing activity. As companies grow by acquisition so more companies will develop into agglomerations or collections of SPUs, supporting a common product portfolio, presented to the market as a cohesive, vertically integrated unit.

For high-volume flow-process manufacture, the trend is towards large, dedicated units supplying a wider market place, so that plants with inherently simple products (such as cigarettes or sheet glass) will supply several countries and face all the problems of language-specific product proliferation and country variants.

As market conditions demand greater product variety at short notice, manufacturing is becoming more complex, both at a strategic (new product introduction) level and at a tactical (day-to-day operations) level. Much strategic planning effort goes into simplifying the logistics, while retaining the benefits of the multinational supply chain. Those who direct and manage these processes must ensure they have the knowledge and skill in their workforce to cope with such complexity. IT could play an important role in supporting these processes.

The other major change to affect manufacturing has been the use of new production methods to maintain the interest of a more educated workforce and to gain the maximum employee effort. Much of the early progress in this area was achieved with quality circles in Japan and this method has since spread to other countries and now involves a wide range of industries and techniques.

Manage the production

Furthermore, the increasing use of sophisticated technologies in industry places the emphasis on managing the production rather than the physical output itself. Industry has the machinery in place to create almost limitless quantities of every product. The real skill of manufacturers is to produce goods profitably and safeguard the future of the company.

Integrated IT in manufacturing

If manufacturers are to break out from their current levels of performance, they will have to apply new concepts of business on a global scale. It is no longer feasible to have a manufacturing process that meets only some of the needs of its customers, nor is it possible to have a research and design programme that is not closely linked to the production and marketing activities of the company. The way forward is not simply investing in IT – only a small competitive gain can be achieved by allowing the various departments of a company to know what the others are doing. Information is not enough and IT is only a part of the answer.

Computer-integrated manufacturing

The key to gaining a competitive edge and building a business for the future is computer-integrated manufacturing (CIM). CIM's origins lie in the development of computer-aided design (CAD), computer-aided manufacturing (CAM) and computer-aided engineering (CAE). It stems from all three disciplines, relies on each of them for key components but still transcends each to produce a wholly new quantum leap in manufacturing possibilities. CIM today is about *integration* of all the functions of a manufacturing business to ensure the right information is available to the right people at the right time and place.

Improving the efficiency of any single department of an organisation may entail the use of CAD, CAM and CAE in some form. Productivity and efficiency in the corporate drawing office may be raised ten-fold by the use of CAD techniques, but the overall efficiency of the organisation may improve by only 5 per cent. The **Total integration** objective of CIM is to use computers to achieve a competitive edge by integrating all aspects of manufacturing and, in this case, to score a proportionally greater increase in efficiency from the use of CAD in the drawing office by linking the improvement with other computer innovations in the company. CIM aims to minimise the need for human intervention in the control of the manufacturing process. CIM embraces all aspects of a manufacturing business from customer order to invoice and from raw material procurement to product delivery.

The practical applications of CIM are limited and much development needs to be done. In a recent study of companies which were moving towards CIM, it became apparent that only 5 per cent of the companies had anything that could be called a significant proportion of a CIM system. This was despite the fact that 60 per cent had made progress in individual technique areas.

Some company units automate their CAD functions and call it CIM. Others concentrate on automating the factory and call that CIM. Still others automate the existing interfaces at current organisational boundaries and use networks, shared databases, communication standards and so on to speed up information flow. Automation of manual processes alone does not constitute CIM. CIM means developing a new way of doing business. The combined requirements create a focused business strategy for streamlining the entire workflow of a business unit.

Taking CIM a step further

Grid analysis is a simple way of clarifying the basic structure of a company. It recognises that all products and manufacturing situations involve variations of two factors: complexity and uncertainty (Figure 20). Capital equipment companies tend to have a relatively high level of both product complexity and uncertainty, as the examples of Nimrod and the Harrier jump jet testify. Commodity businesses tend to have both low complexity (even in complex products such as semiconductors, the technology has advanced to the stage where mass manufacture with minimum defects is now almost routine) and low uncertainty because markets tend to be relatively stable. Fashion or jobbing products tend to have low complexity but high uncertainty, in that they must be timed to match relatively short windows of market opportunity. Consumer durables – particularly goods such as televisions, videos or cars – are becoming steadily more complex, but the demand is long-term and continuous.

In each of these quadrants there will be one or more areas most

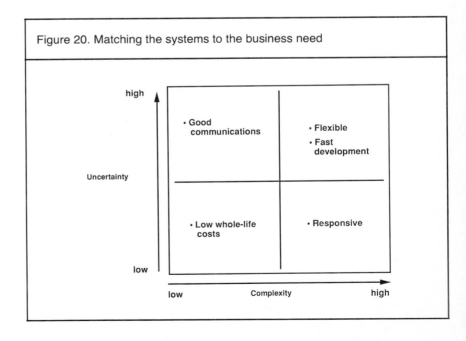

Figure 20. Matching the systems to the business need

likely to produce competitive advantage. In the case of products of high complexity and high market uncertainty, such as a fighter aircraft, then product performance is top of the list. For commodity products, cost is the overriding concern. For fashion products or businesses which are reacting in a jobbing environment, rapid response is the essential feature. In consumer durables, the key aspect is high variety, with a fair degree of product performance, cost sensitivity and quality creeping in as well. These represent a starting point for determining where to invest in CIM. In each case there is a range of CIM techniques and technologies which can be applied to provide significant performance improvements.

CIM a long-term process

CIM is not a product. You cannot rush out to your local IT specialist and buy it for immediate installation. CIM is a strategic approach that takes several years of development. It begins, not with a decision to invest, but with a clear understanding by senior management of what the market in the mid-1990s will look like and what their competitors are likely to be doing then. With this vision of the future at their disposal, management can then begin to build a picture of the technologies they need to create a manufacturing operation that will be competitive in the long term.

The capital goods sector

Capital goods require a very extensive use of CAD and CAE techniques to engineer a complex product which will achieve very high levels of performance. Leading companies in this area often have many home-grown simulation and analysis techniques. (The military aircraft manufacturer will spend millions on a twin-dome combat simulator to squeeze out just a little more performance.) They emphasise computer-aided materials management to control the manufacture and buying-in of materials, parts, sub-assemblies and assemblies, over an extended timescale. Their manufacturing operations emphasise versatile machinery to cope with a huge range of parts produced in small batches on a small number of machines. The tools that CIM will offer a company in this sector are CAD-simulation, materials management and versatile machinery.

The commodities sector

Companies in commodity markets have the option of repositioning their products by adding value (so that they are no longer commodities) or by continuously striving to reduce costs. CAD and CAM can help them develop high quality tooling, patterns and moulds, which will speed production, while efficient management information systems will allow them to keep unit costs under close control. Many process and semi-process businesses fall into this sector. For example, a food manufacturer will use closed-loop process control for each piece of the production line and schedule these with a line control system. A commodity-oriented company would adopt CIM techniques such as process simulation, capacity planning, process control and logistics control.

The consumer goods sector

Companies in consumer durables businesses need to maintain a wide product range, produced in volume within a single plant. Manufacturers of colour televisions, washing machines and automobiles are obvious candidates in this sector for a CIM strategy. This sector is where the Japanese are strongest. Consumer goods groups applying the principles of CIM should opt for careful, modular design (which CAD aids considerably) but should also demand very flexible manufacturing systems, highly efficient and rapid design and very tight Just-In-Time inventory control.

The fashion/jobbing sector

The overriding priority of this sector is the need to respond rapidly to changes in market needs. It needs to focus on swift design and have strict control over production and distribution. Home computer manufacturers fall easily into this category as they are expected to produce new models every year for the main selling period at Christmas. Even a small delay in production during the earlier part of the year can mean their market has been taken over by a rival. The CIM toolkit offers such rapid response companies the ability to excel at rapid design, monitor closely work-in-progress and exercise strict logistics control.

Multiple strategies needed

In practice, many companies operate in several, occasionally all, sectors. The manufacturer of fork-lift trucks may produce a standard range in the durables quadrant, bespoke one-off vehicles in the capital equipment quadrant and spare parts in the jobbing quadrant. Such activities place an overwhelming strain on management, who are in effect running several entirely different businesses simultaneously.

A starting point for CIM

Every company will have its own reasons for adopting CIM. Financial considerations are always prominent and may be any of the following:

- Containing overheads

- Increasing turnover within present staffing levels

- Raising profitability by reducing unit costs

Why wait for a crisis?

Any of these starting points will provide a basis for payback, but most successful schemes are undertaken as a part of an overall market and product strategy. Many companies take this approach because of severe external pressure, such as the threat of closure by the parent company in the USA, an attempt to recover from the loss of a major customer, or the need for breakout performance improvement to face competition from the Far East. But why should it take a major crisis before significant improvements are sought? CIM is a toolkit of techniques and technologies, applied within a clear strategic framework. It involves looking forward, beyond today's technologies to the new technologies that will help achieve the company's strategic goals and that must be allowed for in the design of current systems.

The technologies that underpin CIM are not fixed. They are being added to constantly. Management's view of what is possible and beneficial must also evolve. To provide the discipline needed to maintain the momentum of introducing CIM while allowing sufficient flexibility to draw upon relevant advances in technology, companies must develop competence in specifying and installing CIM systems. Normally, this will mean bringing together business, engineering, production and data-processing experts into a manufacturing technology team.

Picking up the CIM bill

The investment required in management time, capital and training is substantial. One of the key points to recognise is that CIM involves the application of technology to existing organisations. This has two significant implications:

- Some CIM technology is immature. Vendors can supply only a narrow range of products compared with the total needs of

CIM. It has taken CAD/CAM suppliers several decades to reach the point where they can offer adequate solutions to customers. The product range needed for CIM is even larger and scarce skills will be needed to integrate products from a number of vendors.

- The nature of the company must change. Most companies need to change the organisational structure of the firm and retrain staff alongside the introduction of CIM. CIM is not a bandage to cover the company's old festering sores. If the business strategy needs to be re-thought, it had better be re-thought before CIM is contemplated.

The new manufacturing technologies represented by CIM are being described as 'the second industrial revolution'. It will take time for the full impact of this second revolution to be felt.

Why are there so many CIM disaster stories?

Companies introducing CIM frequently experience teething troubles – it can be difficult to implement a radical new approach in an organisation used to more traditional ways. Poor timing, poor selection of the right technologies or lack of commitment are further reasons why CIM sometimes seems to fall short of expectations.

- Poor timing includes investing in technologies before they are proven and moving too late, when the competition is already well ahead. Courageous experiments that did not work include the fully-automated coal mine and the fully automated cigarette-machine factory. Both were defeated by the technology.

- The right technologies must be selected at the outset and they must match the company's needs. A Swedish company spent £5 million on an automated warehouse. But a more effective solution might have been to introduce Just-In-Time techniques and get rid of the warehouse entirely. The key is to look for those parts of the production chain that add value and to invest technology resources there. In this case, storing goods added no value at all.

- Inadequate commitment to CIM can stem from senior management not understanding the implications of the technique and not allocating the right resources at the right time. Companies may also lack the right type of CIM champion to push the strategy through.

Dr Mike Renucci of Jaguar Cars summarised the human element of CIM: 'You can't integrate the technology until you've integrated the people who are using it; you need to bring them all to the party.'

When apparent system failure or poor system performance is examined, it is apparent that most of the problems stem from inadequate attention to managing the transition between manual and automated situations. With CIM the stakes are that much higher. Despite the setbacks, there is an increasing number of manufacturing companies that has scored astonishing success with CIM. Many early successes were in advanced manufacturing industries such as aerospace, automobiles and transport, but CIM has now made strides in chemicals, components, computers, consumer electronics, food and drink, health and personal hygiene products, paper products, pharmaceuticals, process plant, and printing and publishing.

Chrysler's recovery as a force in US car manufacture is partially due to investing in a new CIM-based flexible factory in Detroit. The new technology now allows the company to produce two new models a year instead of one every four years.

Engine manufacturer Lister-Petter halved the design-cycle time for a new product to two years over a five-year period of planned CIM investment. Manning levels fell by a similar proportion, while output was maintained at the same level and inventory greatly reduced.

Austin Rover's high technology centre is a proving ground for new components before full-scale production. Part of a £600 million investment in CIM, the centre has been responsible for, among other things, cutting the toolroom development time on new cylinder heads by two-thirds. Design modifications that used to take weeks now take hours, allowing a much more rapid response to market needs.

Jaguar Cars will use CAD and CAM exclusively for all design, analysis and tooling for its new model, due to be launched in the early 1990s. These techniques will save at least two years on development lead time.

The consumer electronics sector, which has seen product lives drop from an average of around three years to as little as three months, has embraced CIM. Faced with this type of competition, it is no longer enough to have one generation of product in production and one about to be launched. Now a third, and possibly a fourth, needs to be waiting in the wings.

Flexibility improvements

Manufacturing flexibility is required for a number of reasons, including:

- Changes in the market and the need to maintain market momentum with new products
- Changes in technology that reduce cost or improve the product
- Using one factory to produce a number of standard products that may vary in sales volume

Whereas large, dedicated production machines can usually produce at lower unit cost than smaller more flexible machines, they rely heavily on minimum change in the product. They also rely on accuracy in the forecasting of demand. Neither of these factors can be guaranteed in a single market. Moreover, the cost of changing a production line is often prohibitive. CIM provides the necessary flexibility.

Quality improvements

Total Quality Management (TQM) has promoted the idea that customers buy quality products and that quality products are produced by organisations in which everything is dominated by quality. TQM is a key component of CIM and together they can:

- Enable the designer to analyse a new design more thoroughly
- Ensure process plans are suited to the production facilities available
- Provide tracking of purchased materials throughout production and distribution to monitor supplier performance
- Support statistical process control by automating the tasks involved in monitoring quality on the shop floor

Hewlett-Packard has argued that quality and productivity are synonymous in practical terms; that improving the former automatically improves the latter. It cites, for example, its Japanese subsidiary, where the failure rate in wave soldering has been reduced from 500 per million in 1978 to 2 per million in 1986. And the subsidiary is working on reducing the failure rate still further!

Cost improvements

Just-In-Time

A wide range of costs can be reduced by the application of CIM. The classic approach to inventory reduction is Just-In-Time, which has, in some cases, cut inventory by 50 per cent or more. Just-In-Time is most effective where demand is relatively stable and where a wide range of products pass through a single plant. Tandem Computer applied computerised Just-In-Time to a plant producing 170 printed circuit boards (with one new type being added every other day). Apart from cutting a nineteen-week production cycle to nine days, they have also reduced inventory by 50 per cent, doubled throughput with less floorspace and substantially increased manpower productivity.

In the past, automation has reduced the need for unskilled labour by taking over repetitive operations. The major effect of CIM on staff levels is to remove the need for manual data handling at clerical, supervisory and middle management levels. Electronic data interchange with customers and suppliers removes many clerical tasks. It should not be forgotten that it costs about £10 to send a document manually.

People improvements

Enhances creativity

In many organisations, CIM has enhanced the creative skills of people affected by the changes. One reason for this is that people now have a much wider perspective on what is happening with the business because information is more transparent and available. At the same time, job specifications tend to be wider and more demanding of specialist skills and training. CIM enables creative designers and imaginative managers to achieve high performance more consistently.

Automates repetitive tasks

It also removes repetitive, low skill jobs from the system. Automating repetitive tasks tends to reduce errors and free people to do more interesting and valuable jobs for the company. Because CIM crosses all disciplines, it brings additional benefits in the form of helping to focus strategic thinking in all functional areas in the same direction.

Health warning

The early history of automation has largely been a process of replacing people with computerised machines. The next stage will be achieved by linking islands of automation across the organisation. The key word in CIM is integration. A clear understanding of the company's needs for integration has to underlie all decisions of technology purchase, systems, database design and organisational restructuring. Integration is easiest with mature technologies which are reasonably well known and well understood and most difficult with technologies that are still developing, such as expert systems. Many of the tools with the greatest potential are the most recent and the least mature. There is a danger that companies will invest heavily in the wrong technologies.

The techniques and technologies that make up CIM span all the major business functions, from collection and interpretation of customer information to distribution. Some set out to improve the effectiveness of specific functions. Others are more to do with integrating the activities of several functions. However, every company is different and each will require its own unique style of CIM.

Process of continual improvement

The multinational supply chain is concerned with the link between factory and customer on the one hand and supplier and factory on the other. Factories currently tend to be product-focused and the emphasis is on simplifying an inherently complex logistics chain by:

- The use of semi-autonomous SPUs

- Minimising the flow of materials between factories

- Strong central product planning and co-ordination functions

- The use of low inventory, fast response manufacturing to reduce the forecasting problem (both in terms of demand and cost fluctuations)

- An emphasis on highly predictable, co-ordinated delivery

The organisation that can manifest all these attributes together will enjoy significant commercial advantage.

With CIM, instead of taking a one-shot effort at implementing this strategy, a company can introduce it gradually so that it can be managed properly and so that early gains can be made. CIM is not a once only exercise. It is part of a new culture of continuous improvement.

It is important to recognise that the world will move on during the implementation of a three- or five-year plan, especially with the many changes associated with the single market. The goals of the company may need to change and the strategy may need to be redefined to meet the new goals. The CIM strategy will need to be fine-tuned annually to meet changes in such factors as:

- The objectives and direction of the business

- The state of the market

- Changing suppliers

- Advances in technology

- The current capabilities (including investment constraints) of clients

The CIM strategy will also evolve following reviews of the progress of CIM projects and assessments of the merits of completed work. CIM is still in its infancy. It requires rare skills and a radical attitude for successful implementation. Before CIM is widely accepted a number of important changes must take place:

- A new breed of CIM engineers must be created. They will need to be familiar with IT, machines and the manufacturing business.

- A new class of modular CIM products must be built to data and communication standards so that they can be easily adapted for each installation.

- A new visionary attitude among board members is necessary since the introduction of CIM can only be tackled in the context of a restructured business.

The factory of the future is taking shape and many of the components vital to staging a breakthrough into a new form of industrial revolution are already in place. The single market will bring to the fore the phenomenal potential of IT when it is fully integrated with the manufacturing and distribution processes.

7.   The office of the future

Within the next decade, technology will bring about more profound changes in the office than in the factory or home because there has been so little change in the way offices have operated over the past two hundred years. As the factory has gradually evolved into today's automated production line and the home has taken full advantage of devices and techniques to make life easier and more comfortable, the office has remained in a backwater, starved of investment and relying on the goodwill of white-collar workers to keep the wheels turning.

The computer appeared in its first commercial form in the 1950s working primarily on numeric data and technical analysis. Its primary justification in financial terms was its value in detailed analysis. By the 1960s and 1970s, computer application had shifted to automating transactions, using transaction processing technology, and was applied in the operational side of the organisation. Here the justification was simple cost saving over existing manual methods. In the 1980s, a new phase of computer use developed as the huge volumes of data that were captured electronically were deemed to have a strategic value. The concept of information systems evolved and investment was made in databases, networks and decision support tools. The justification for these systems was one of strategy rather than immediate benefit.

An important conclusion which can be drawn from this thirty-year period of growth is that current systems are based on the architecture of data-processing designed to support highly structured activities – transaction processing. This architecture will need to change if it is to provide business with the necessary tools to support entry into European and global markets.

UK loses its leading position with information systems

A decade ago, the UK enjoyed a leading position in the take-up of office systems. The technology at the time was still relatively immature and the explosion in the use of personal computers had not yet taken place. With a strong lead from the Department of Trade and Industry and valuable support from the Computer Services Association, a unique skills base was developed, initially with early investigations of the benefits of word-processing and then with a pilot programme of introducing office systems in the public sector.

Unfortunately some of the facilities introduced early in 1982 under the pilot schemes – work group computing, voice storage and forward, voice annotation of documents, information storage and retrieval, compound document production, videotext, fibre optic links and homeworking – have still not moved beyond an embryonic stage in many UK organisations. Even more regrettable is the fact that other countries have since taken up some of these technologies and are aggressively promoting them to build a strong domestic IT industry.

A similar lead in the effective implementation of systems has been lost as organisations in both the private and public sectors have failed to move beyond the pilot phase to implement good corporate IT systems. Organisation blocks have slowed development down. As a result, it is difficult to find positive reference sites for good end-user computer systems in the UK today. Users, suppliers and consultants alike have failed in their efforts to get first-class systems operational. A lack of commitment from the top, both nationally and locally, has meant that the brief lead we had in adopting IT has been lost. Instead of being a world-class exporter of such technology, the UK is now a net importer of hardware and software on a very large scale. Even our lead in software development and services has been lost to European, particularly French, rivals, who have been aggressive in building or acquiring software companies. Unlike the French sorties into the UK water industry, the loss of our software companies passed by with hardly a comment.

Rather than using our leading position to consolidate our manufacturing, software development and computing services, we now have a fragmented series of sub-industries, none of which can claim to be a force in Europe today. Whereas other countries seem to accept the need for strategic corporate alliances, we are still waiting for British Telecom, ICL, Amstrad and the UK computing services industry to establish a credible UK force in European computing and communications. Although we may already have lost the lead in the manufacture of IT systems, it will be devastating to UK industry as a whole if we become a second-rate user of these systems.

The pace of technology development has quickened in the last decade and many of the technical options now open to organisations are relatively new (Figure 21). In many cases, the knowledge-base of organisations is built upon out-of-date ideas of what computer tech-

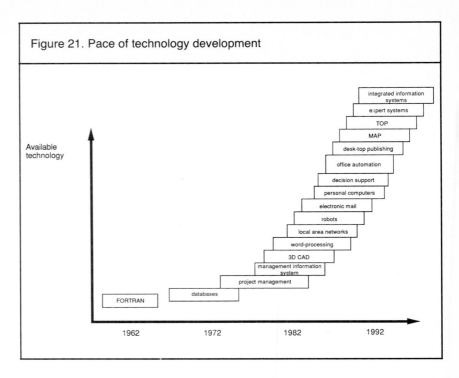

Figure 21. Pace of technology development

nology can offer. FORTRAN may have been the cutting edge of IT in the early 1960s, but much has happened in the meantime. Management has a responsibility to keep abreast of the latest developments in IT.

Paperless office a myth

The spread of computers in general and in IT in particular over the past two decades has been accompanied by the popular concept of the paperless office. Some companies have set this as their primary goal in implementing an IT programme because it is seen as one of the best ways to achieve huge productivity gains. The paperless office, however, is a myth. Most companies that institute an IT system discover to their shock that in some key areas their reliance on paper-based activity has actually increased, even though they have shifted the emphasis of their communications investment into electronics.

Pulp and paper producers will confirm that the total office paper market has increased over the last decade but the nature of the paper used has changed. Computer printouts, which are not a very efficient or manageable form of presenting data, now represent a huge element of office paper supplies. This says something about how IT professionals are supporting their 'clients'. Over 150,000 tonnes of continuous stationery is used in the UK every year and demand is estimated to continue to rise at a rate of about 30 per cent a year. The general business supplies of uncoated wood-free printing and writing papers is growing at about 5 per cent a year and amounts to 1 million tonnes, while cut-size paper for photocopiers and office stationery is growing at 10 per cent a year. There will always be a need for a hard copy of a computer screen image, but paper as a percentage of office communications should decline as the pace of electronic business activity increases in domestic and world markets, and as the quality of the electronic support systems improve.

Technical improvements

Since the early 1970s, IT has recorded phenomenal technical improvements in performance. Exponential growth in processing power, incredible reductions in size and a bewildering range of new functional capabilities have characterised the industry in the recent past and are set to continue into the next century. Accompanying these technological leaps and bounds has been a virtual free-fall in price. Home computers are common, while the electronic content of many domestic appliances has soared. This improved range of applications has done much to enhance the public image of computer processing technology and has given IT a toehold in the collective subconscious of the public.

As product power, range and applications have jumped, so too has productivity growth where computers – and IT in particular – have been employed, especially in the area of structured applications such as payroll and personnel. On the other hand, productivity improvements in the less structured areas around managerial and professional activity have been less impressive despite large investment in personal computers. Productivity gains are not easy to realise.

1992 will raise the stakes

The role of the office

In the run-up to 1992, the role of the office will undergo a series of searching examinations. Organisations will need to redefine roles and responsibilities as they form their European outlook. There will be a greater need for guidance, counselling and coaching of staff and management alike. At the same time there will be a fundamental questioning of why people go to an office and whether the formal definition of an office is still valid. Large organisations which have built up huge office administrations will be the hardest hit in this review, while smaller, relatively unsophisticated businesses will be able to by-pass the current office infrastructures and move straight into the 1990s with extensive IT support.

New office systems will need to be:

- Usable

- Relevant to users

- Provide access to needed information

- Flexible

- Expandable

- Supportable

In order to meet the demands of the coming decade, the systems will need to be simple enough to operate without restricting 'enthusiastic' users too much. And although technically sophisticated systems are not necessary, technically sound systems are essential. Management must be allowed to see immediate returns on their investment, so systems will need to deliver some value to the company quickly, thereby maintaining interest and co-operation for future gains. A small network of word processors and personal computers is unlikely to be a recipe for success in hard European market conditions.

Information delivery

**Superior
infrastructure**

The delivery and monitoring of decisions is a crucial area of management concern. It is no longer safe to assume that a 'good' decision will be accepted by the rest of the organisation. People need to be persuaded, supported or threatened to make them take the important step from decision to action, and behaviour needs to be monitored to ensure that no regression takes place. Information delivery will become a key issue for organisations in the next decade. Those that wish to excel will require a superior information delivery infrastructure.

Unstructured activities make change more difficult

Over the past thirty years, organisations have automated many operational roles and IT has fuelled the growth of less structured thinking roles among management, professionals and knowledge workers. The stable environment of the 1950s that operated largely structured activities on a limited information base has been fundamentally changed into a more dynamic environment which operates more unstructured roles that are supported by a vastly increased information resource. During this period, the number of people employed in offices has increased dramatically from 30 per cent to almost 50 per cent of the entire UK workforce.

Automation/systems   The office of the future will doubtless operate with a mixture of structured and unstructured activities. This is where it becomes necessary to distinguish between office automation and office systems. Office automation applies technology designed to support transaction processing to the automation of discrete activities in the office, while office systems support the process by which people work within the office and allow them to use the technology in any way they desire. This distinction will grow in importance as we move closer to 1992 and the need for flexibility of office activities increases.

The future office environment, which will operate a combination of data processing technology to support the structured activities and information systems support for unstructured activities, will be characterised by three architectural components:

- Acquisition of information

- Assimilation of information

- Communication of information

The second and third components are perhaps the most difficult to automate since they involve the more creative side of staff and the thinking portion of the work. IT, however, can make the interpretation of information easier and facilitate the swift and clear communication of conclusions. Information does not flow neutrally up the organisation but is filtered at successive levels. IT systems can reduce the filtering effect by encouraging more direct contact between disparate levels.

A consistent information architecture

If a company is to derive maximum benefits from integrated office systems with communication between people in different locations, a consistent information architecture becomes necessary. Depending on the nature of the organisation, this may mean a consistent document interchange format, which in the past has required the selection of a single proprietary system and the use of the suppliers' com-

Open standards

munications standards to achieve interchange. It is possible to achieve interchange between diverse supplier systems but usually only after great difficulty and considerable expense. The current transition towards internationally agreed open standards will make effective document interchange easier.

These standards are complex and the standards-making process is slow, relative to technical developments in the computer industry. This places the onus on companies to do much of the work themselves to establish their own integrated network. Document interchange is only the bottom rung of the interchange ladder and to be really effective it is necessary for a network to be used in the same manner by many people at many different locations. This requires the establishment of a common and agreed language – and this may be as difficult to achieve as the technical interworking.

A consistent and effective user interface

It is important to ensure that the user interface is consistent. The Apple Macintosh interface has until recently differed from the majority of personal computer and workstation interfaces. It imposed a consistent easy-to-use interface on a variety of facilities. It is more effective than a system where users have to learn different interfaces for different activities as they do with many other personal computer systems. The quality of the user interfaces generally is improving rapidly. It will not be long before an acceptable interface is available for major integrated office-system installations.

A good integrated office system provides an effective link with the traditional data processing or management information system (MIS) facilities. The office system does not replace them but it will draw information from these systems. Maintaining the integrity of the information and protecting its security will be important tasks. Achieving the balance of control and responsibility between the central MIS function and the end-user departments will be one of the most difficult tasks facing organisations in their preparation for the single market.

Multi-cultural applications

The office of 1992 will need to cope with differences in language, currency and culture. The accounts department will need to handle multi-currency invoicing; the marketing department will have to produce sales literature in at least three other languages; support services will have to be provided in each country where products are sold; the sales force will need to be trained and equipped to offer an effective and speedy service that addresses local cultural variations; senior management will need performance data on each operating unit, and some pan-European measure of performance will need to be developed or accepted such as the European currency unit (ecu).

The journey towards reaching the office of the future will require a new emphasis on integrating formerly disparate components of the organisation so that they work more effectively. This integration will not in itself create competitive advantage but it will facilitate it. Integrated information systems enable people to deliver better services and new products more quickly at a lower cost and with more certainty than their competitors.

Sales and marketing in Europe

A new range of sales and marketing techniques will have to be employed if UK industry is to take advantage of the opportunities that the single market offers.

It is possible to learn from some of the harsh lessons that the computer industry itself had to endure when trying to meet the different types of culture in country after country. In the UK, for example, a company's head office is never very far from its customer base – perhaps a maximum of a four-hour car journey. Direct selling can be achieved relatively easily and at a reasonable cost. Whereas the size of the UK might be equal to that of one of the larger states in the USA, most of our industrial, financial and government functions operate from the South East.

West Germany, because of its federal political structure, has its population and businesses dispersed throughout the entire country. So IBM, for example, has to operate a totally different supplier–service network in West Germany to the one it operates in the south-east of England, where two-thirds of its mainframe business is concentrated. This suggests that foreign companies are going to find it easier to establish business in the UK than UK firms will in any single national market.

Using information to provide superior service

The demands placed by customers on the services offered by a company are likely to increase in proportion to the distance between the market and true source of supply. A manufacturer with a single plant in south-east England may find it difficult to compete with a competitor which has distributed office throughout Europe, especially if the sales force has been put into the field fully equipped with strong lines of communication back to the home base.

It may only take ten or twelve people on the road to establish an efficient European network, but if these people are unreliable, or their communications are inadequate, or their cars keep breaking down, or they are unable to furnish customers with the right information, product or services, the customer will look beyond them to their existing home base to resolve queries, get new prices or negotiate terms. On the other hand, if the sales force excels in all of these areas and can deal quickly with any problem that a real or potential customer might have, it will become irrelevant where the home base is located in Europe. If a company can establish a quality infrastructure (and IT's role in this is vital), it will be able to supply a diverse geographical area with little alteration to its own structure.

Technology can overcome geography

The Golden Circle

The greatest concentration of wealth, population, business activity and commercial opportunity within the EC lies in the north east, in a triangle from London through Brussels, across the Netherlands in northern Germany and down south into the Frankfurt/Strasbourg region. The region which is within a 250-mile radius of Cologne has been termed 'the Golden Circle' by advertising agency D'Arcy Masius Benton & Bowles because it contains 50 million relatively wealthy consumers. While this may offer a much larger catchment area than the south-east of England, it has already matured as a market from decades of bitter commercial competition. This will hardly be a joy ride for any UK company, but it would represent a logical first move in establishing a European sales and marketing foothold before moves are made into, say, Italy or southern Europe.

Sales and marketing in Europe will absorb vast quantities of management time and the cost of running a number of offices that have little opportunity for integration across national boundaries can be high. Phased expansion is a more sensible approach. Brussels could act as the first element in a European sales and marketing network since English is widely spoken and a large number of international companies are already headquartered there. The city is a relatively short distance from London, Paris and the Ruhr.

Phased expansion

Once branch offices are established beyond this beach-head, the logistics become difficult. France is dominated by the Paris region, but smaller secondary markets such as Lyons and Marseilles exist. In Italy, the establishment of a Turin or Milan office will cover the main industrial north, but the political and financial heart of the country lies

600 miles to the south in Rome, while southern Italy has a large programme of EC development aid.

Purchasing and accounts on a European scale

Purchasing

Just as sales and marketing will need a new approach, the purchasing function in the 1992 office will require a new strategy to cope with far-ranging market changes. The traditional approach to purchasing requires achievement of six 'rights' – the right item, at the right price, at the right time, at the right quality, in the right quantity, from the right supplier. We must now add the right technology infrastructure.

For many companies, the single market will cause profound changes in the ways they operate and the products and services they supply. Purchasers in retailing will be buying new items to suit new markets or to cater for changes in their existing markets. Manufacturing companies will need to purchase new components for new products or for products that are being modified or rationalised for the new markets. As UK companies move towards 1992, the purchasing function will become more complex as product variety increases, particularly if promotional material and packaging are required in several languages.

Factors affecting price

Several factors will affect prices: increased competition among suppliers will lower prices; de-regulation will increase the tempo of this competition; the removal of borders will cut logistics costs and this can be passed on to customers in lower delivered costs; and national companies will be aiming to achieve economies of scale by buying *en bloc* rather than separately.

Meeting the 'right time' requirement will be made easier for international purchases as border delays are eliminated and journey times are reduced and made more reliable, both of which will allow a Just-In-Time supply policy.

Standards are becoming more uniform across Europe as BS 5750 and ISO 9000 are being applied. The increasing trend to use quality to provide a competitive edge, already evident in the car, food and electrical goods industries, will spread to other sectors as competition increases. The purchasing function has a part to play in developing quality and reducing its cost. Note, however, that programmes have achieved considerable cost reductions as a result of a search for quality, not the other way around. The quality programme should, therefore, be the driver for change.

Purchasing on a European scale

The 'right quantity' may change. As national companies within existing multinational organisations review their European purchasing strategies, they will discover that some items are bought more effectively on a European scale. Economies of scale can be achieved by buying total European volumes together, particularly when the items are traded on European or world markets rather than national markets. Some international companies negotiate single worldwide contracts with international suppliers but with local call-offs against these contracts.

Improved purchasing power is one benefit which can arise from a merger or acquisition if the new partners have items they purchase or suppliers in common.

Choice of suppliers

The 'right supplier' may differ after 1992 because a wider choice of accessible suppliers will exist as borders are removed, existing suppliers may offer a wider range of goods and services to their home market, some suppliers will cease to trade because they are uncompetitive, mergers and acquisitions will take place among suppliers, and because local suppliers may have difficulty meeting local demand as they market their goods abroad.

As 1992 approaches, the purchasing function within organisations will change because of the changes in the structure of the rest of the company and because it will have to change if it is to be more effective in helping the company achieve profitability and competitiveness.

Accounts

If the single market is going to offer opportunities for economies of scale in the purchasing of goods, there are also going to be changes in how those goods are requested and paid for. The need to cope with multi-currency invoicing is going to create some problems, but equally important will be the existence of different bands of VAT. In the UK we have had a single VAT rate for many years. There are some exceptions (such as the additional tax on cars) but, by and large, we have a simple system. In other countries the situation is more complicated, with two or even three bands of VAT. It is to be hoped that current information systems can cope with these variations, and show the complexity of liabilities for tax in the different member states.

Paperless trading

Another, perhaps more important, impact on the accounts departments of companies in the UK will be made by increasing paperless trading. With the reduction or elimination of trade barriers, much of the very complex paper work which is currently generated for customs purposes should be eliminated. This will mean that the major transactions will become concentrated in the purchase order and invoicing procedures between companies. There has already been a great deal of progress in simplifying and speeding up such transactions (known as Value-Added and Data Services or VADS, or Electronic Data Interchange or EDI). Any company that wishes to present an efficient image to its customers and suppliers should be exploring the benefits of these technology developments.

Research

Cross-functional communication

Significant changes will take place in the field of research (whether market research, competitor research, or product research) as the impact of the single market is felt throughout UK industry. We have already discussed how R&D will have to respond to the new intense market conditions by being able to identify new products and processes that have world market potential and by developing the mechanisms and systems to transfer these to the market as quickly as possible. Today's prevalent sequenced approach will be replaced by parallel working with cross-functional teams being used to operate from product conception to market entry. An effective IT system will be essential to aid this cross-functional communication and to support the process from R&D through to product launch.

The importance of infrastructure

As companies establish more of a European market presence, it will be important for the IT infrastructure to keep pace. Integrated support systems and teleworking will not operate if there is not the network to support them. This may be a public pan-European telecommunications network, an in-company network or a managed network service. Companies will have to choose between them.

Telecommunications in Europe

The Commission has made opening up telecommunications services and terminal equipment to competition a priority in its moves to create the single market. Despite opposing political positions within the Community, the trend towards telecommunications liberalisation is now clear: the question is not whether policies and regulations will change, but how quickly and by how much. 1992 will be one of a series of mileposts rather than a single changeover point.

Monopoly in the basic telecommunications network has been jealously guarded by the traditionally monopolistic national telecommunications authorities (TAs). The most significant breach so far is in the UK, with the creation of the duopoly of BT and Mercury. The competition engendered has unquestionably driven down prices and encouraged technological advances, delivering improved services, in particular to such communications-intensive sectors as the financial services industry.

ISDN

Network competition and technology are inter-related. All European TAs are installing broadband (very high capacity) links and digital exchanges in the Public Switched Telephone Network (PSTN), and are moving towards the Integrated Services Digital Network (ISDN). ISDN is capable of handling digital voice and data over the same switched public network, taking advantage of the convergence of computing and telecommunications and delivering services which cannot be made available over existing networks. ISDN can bring a new degree of freedom in the choice of locations and the relationships between them.

Cable TV

Management must also be aware of the alternatives to the traditional fixed network. One is cable television, which is capable of delivering both conventional voice telephony and broadband business services as well as entertainment. This is particularly important in countries such as the Netherlands, where cable penetration of households is greater than 70 per cent. National approaches range from integrating the networks, to the UK's approach, where the TAs are currently debarred from offering entertainment television, and cable operators can offer telecommunications only in conjunction with a TA. Whichever regulatory route is followed, the wide availability of broadband end-user connections, cost-justified on entertainment services, has important implications for business.

Cellular radio

Mobile systems also present new dimensions to working in Europe. Cellular radio has proved an enormous commercial success, transforming the working habits of the busy self-employed plumber as much as the chief executive. It is significant that both growth-rate and decline in real costs to the user are greatest in the UK, where two cellular operators and a separate tier of airtime retailers compete. The technical standards for a pan-European system covering at least sixteen countries are agreed, and development is well advanced. This is an excellent example of technology-led success fuelled by competition.

One of the most important new developments in which the UK leads is Telepoint (CT2). This allows a user to make calls within a short distance – 100 to 150 metres – of a fixed service point. The handsets are substantially lighter and cheaper than cellular radio units, and use of the radio spectrum is incomparably more economical. UK operators are already committed to the development of a Common Air Interface (CAI) which will permit 'roaming' between service providers, and strong pressure for Europe-wide standards is part of the 1992 initiative. The importance of CT2 is as a personal communicator. In the home, it is the complete cordless telephone. At work, it becomes a cordless Private Automatic Branch Exchange (PABX) extension, with everything that implies for office management and layout. Anywhere within reach of a low cost tele-point connected to the PSTN, the personal communicator can replace inherently expensive cellular systems and remove reliance on the fixed telephone. From the point of view of the TA, elimination of the expensive 'last kilometre' alters the basic economics of networks. This transformation of the way we will communicate relies on a market which is unified in the fullest sense to deliver its benefits.

Value Added and Data Services (VADS) in Europe

VADS, a generic term covering a range of services, deal with the exchange of structured business information. They are a method of carrying business information using computer systems to create networks which exploit the advantages of accuracy, speed, and guaranteed delivery, at an acceptable cost.

Economical information exchange

There are many reasons why VADS have proved attractive to a variety of market sectors. One of the major ones is the elimination of unnecessary activities. Estimates suggest that as much as 70 per cent of inter-company computer output is re-entered into other computers. Not only is this time-consuming, but re-entry is a potential source of error. Finding the source of the error and rectifying it leads to additional, and even more expensive, inter-company communication. Today many companies are exchanging information on orders, invoices, delivery schedules and funds transfer electronically and are consequently benefiting from staff and time savings, reduced postal costs and delays, and elimination of errors.

VADS networks can be established between a group of companies who have a close trading relationship, or they can be established by a third party who offers it as a service. What is important is that the trading partners work to common, agreed standards, so interchange of information can take place between different computer systems. Because of this, it has been easier to establish VADS when structured data is involved. Provided there are a limited range of structured fields (such as name and address, account and purchase order numbers, delivery date, and financial details), then interchange is possible, even though the sending and receiving computer systems may use different internal formats for structuring the information. The common interchange format ensures consistency.

The launch in 1982 by Thomson's of a nationwide reservation system using viewdata terminals had a profound impact on the travel trade's use of IT. Most of the other companies had to respond rapidly with their own systems so that just three years later over 90 per cent of ABTA travel agents were using viewdata terminals. This indicates how powerful an advantage electronic links can be and should serve as a warning in the context of 1992. Ten years previously, firms that were not aggressive in their use of IT lost market share in the travel sector.

What is important is for groups of companies to evaluate the potential benefits of establishing such links. This is an area where no one company can 'go it alone', and the UK has been at the forefront in the exploitation of VADS. It is an area where it will be vital to maintain the lead in the run-up to 1992. The selective extension of the links into Europe could provide an important competitive advantage for UK companies.

Information in-flows

Individual departments will need greatly increased flows of improved information if the company is to meet the challenge of the single market. Many of the information types that are needed are common across departments:

- Financial information to provide the background and rationale behind a project so that priorities can be established. Access to up-to-date budgetary control data will also mean effort remains focused.

- Operational information to illustrate the effectiveness of previous work and to identify future areas of activity.

- Information from within the company or externally to eliminate duplication of effort. Systems also need to be developed to capture information from previous company employees in the form of an expert- or knowledge-based system.

- Market information to help to define customer needs.

- Access to information on external companies to identify potential suppliers, customers and competitors.

Information out-flows

The output of reports, data and analyses will be facilitated by desk-top publishing. Financial data as to the value of activities will be available from an analysis of current and historical data, while communication of all the information will be speeded up through networks.

Supporting business applications

There are many applications of IT that will aid business development. They include:

- Decision analysis techniques to reaffirm that the choice of project undertaken by the department is relevant to the overall business goal

- Modelling techniques to speed up the project and reduce the costs of mistakes

- The ability to test alternatives and to investigate the financial consequences of specific courses of action

- Financial analysis of the project to make line management aware of the financial implications of any work and enable constant monitoring of the project's relevance to the overall business strategy

- Project control techniques to enable work to be kept on time and within budget

- Expert systems which offer great potential for improving performance

The benefits of an effective Euro-office infrastructure

The benefits that companies have realised through the considered use of integrated information systems, VADS and in-company electronic networks is an indication of the benefits that can be realised in many areas of a company from the use of IT.

Quality

Integrated systems eliminate the errors that can result from the manual transcription of details. Companies can also establish further improvements in quality using electronic links. Increasingly, companies are not just ordering goods, they are ordering goods of a certain quality to be delivered on a certain date. How well a company meets the performance criteria (whether in delivery reliability, reject rate or specifications) can be assessed more easily as a result of the improvement in management information brought about by the integrated systems.

Efficiency and effectiveness

The elimination of activities which do not add value to the production process, the reduction in stock levels, minimisation of wastage, and the avoidance of additional communication to rectify errors are all ways in which improvements can be realised.

Responsiveness

By using integrated information systems it is possible to deliver a faster and higher quality of service to customers, and to avoid situations where their needs cannot be met (letting goods go out of stock, for example). Sales people can be sure of delivery dates, prices, special discounts, and the history of the customer relationship, if the sales database has qualitative as well as quantitative information.

Customer service

As well as speed of service, it is possible to offer additional services on some occasions. Frequent flyers may well have details of their preferences for smoking or non-smoking, window or aisle seats, in the system, so that no matter who books the seat, satisfaction is ensured.

Unless the white-collar activities which form such a large part of any company's cost base can deliver benefits similar to those that will be realised by CIM, then UK organisations will have a significant handicap in competing in the single market. Management attention must be directed towards improving both CIM and integrated information systems (IIS). Like CIM, IIS require a cultural shift within the organisation, they require executive input for overall direction, and a managed evolution towards ever better systems supporting the overall business strategy. The 1992 developments will force organisation to pay greater attention to the quality of their information systems, and the drive for improvements must come from the very top of the organisation.

8.　The non-technical components of success

'There are three ways to ruin yourself: gambling, women and technology. Gambling is the fastest, women are the most pleasurable, and technology is the most certain.' *Georges Pompidou*

The challenge that the single market offers UK industry is great. In one single process, UK management will have to redirect its focus towards half a dozen major markets, learn how to compete in numerous languages and cultures, deliver products and services that offer sustainable competitive advantage, lock in existing domestic customers, ward off overwhelming competition from Continental Europe, throw out one set of computer principles and adopt a viable reliance on IT, continue to motivate staff and, most of all, continue to trade profitably.

The single market will not be an instant occurrence like metrication was, nor even the two- or three-year process that new entrants to the EC experience before becoming full members. Instead it will be a profound long-term process that coincides with one of the most important technological quantum leaps since the industrial revolution. It is, therefore, vital that management takes a long-term view of any change process and acts in the short term to ensure long-term success. The quality of management and the framework management adopts in approaching a change situation will be vital components in determining the overall outcome – in the short, medium and long terms.

Executive disappointment

IT has a poor public relations record among senior management. Disappointment has been particularly prevalent in the UK, compared with France or West Germany. It has stemmed from delays, backlogs and cost overruns. IT supporters have too frequently oversold the possible benefits of their technology, while management has been too ready to assume that the success the company has had in non-operational systems, such as payroll, stock control and personnel, is a guide to what they can expect from the more sophisticated and more costly technological jump towards computer-integrated information systems.

Reluctance to change

The biggest single obstacle to organisations' progress in developing effective information systems is the belief that they are already in place. Much of the infrastructure of any company is there to prevent fresh innovation unsettling existing policies and procedures, purchasing restrictions and power bases. An executive reluctance to change means that rearguard actions are sometimes set in motion to ensure minimal progress for any project that is deemed to be threatening. European industry has gained enormously from factory automation and change has become a way of life, but few companies adopt the same commitment to IT for its white-collar workers. Instead, passive resistance to IT is undertaken to sap the energy from a project: a committee is established, a fully evaluated pilot or prototype is requested, or a postponement is sought until the company's bottom line improves. This goes part of the way to explaining why few senior managers use computer terminals – yet there has been an explosion in the use of cellular radios by this same group of people because they pose no threat, offer no change to working habits and require no new skills. To overcome these inherent obstacles requires the dedication of a project champion. They, unfortunately, are a rare breed.

Developing a framework for change

Ask the right questions

Many of the recent disappointments with IT have arisen not because the technology failed to work in the manner expected but because there was no obvious effect on organisational performance. Underlying this problem has been an inability to ask the right questions early enough. Management has seldom asked the fundamental questions of what goes on in their organisations and why certain things happen before analysing the potential benefits of computerisation. Here the old adage rings true: 'If you automate a mess, all you get is an automated mess in which things go wrong faster.'

Because the costs of technology have been pushed down dramatically, people and organisations seek ways to apply this technology without questioning whether it is needed, or where and how much of it is needed. Without adequate prior analysis, few benefits are derived, the systems are used less frequently and the systems department that installed them suffers a loss of credibility.

Although they have been neglected by the world of computers, there exists a well-established set of principles which can be applied to any situation in which change occurs. Much of the organisation theory of the last forty years has focused on how to get major changes introduced into organisations more effectively.

Involvement a cornerstone of success

'You have to change the way people think in order to manage change, and you have to give people time to make changes.' So observed the CEO of a small high-precision engineering company in the USA that decided to automate its entire factory and integrate most of the engineering functions through IT.

The company outlined five simple rules to guide its IT programme:

- If it does not have a business purpose, do not do it

- If it does not follow the business plan, do not do it

- If if does not pay for itself, do not do it

- If it cannot be explained in English, do not do it

- If it cannot be explained in physical operations terms, do not do it

The company realised that when it began its automation programme, it could not automate a little at a time. In order to minimise the long-term disruption of automating the entire company, it was decided to automate as quickly as possible – over a weekend. By installing an integrated manufacturing system in a few days to handle both office and factory work, they did not have to rely on parallel operations of old accounting and inventory control systems. This proved stressful at first, but it was less disruptive to the company and the employees over the long term.

Educate staff

The company concentrated on educating its staff. Former machine operators, who would be programming and maintaining robots and lathes in the new regime, were sent to classes in algebra and trigonometry in local colleges. The entire company took classes in quality control. Vendors were also involved in hardware and software tuition. Everyone became involved in the changes. Every piece of equipment on the shop floor was installed by the people who were going to operate it. Every job in the company changed and most were expanded to take in several jobs. This gave the shop floor the flexibility to produce more custom orders at short notice.

Educate suppliers and customers

Education was extended to vendors, customers and bankers. The company talked to over 200 vendors before finding the right system and on many of the field trips, long-standing customers were brought along to be shown the type of change that the company was attempting. On other trips, the company's bankers were taken along, so they could see the scope of the investment decisions.

Within three years, the company had tripled production with the same number of staff, had boosted machine utilisation from 14 per cent to 70 per cent and had doubled output per employee to $160,000 compared with a national average of $77,000. The workforce had stabilised and lead times were down to two weeks from twelve weeks.

The non-technical factors for success

There is more to a successful IT programme than technology. This is clearly evinced by programme post-mortems, which discover that failure or underperformance of IT strategies seldom relate to the hardware or software being used. More often than not there are human and organisational dimensions that do not allow the real benefits of an IT programme to flow through to the business.

The evolution of technology and the evolution of understanding large-scale organisation of change have taken separate paths so that different parts of a company will view the same event in radically different ways. Much is known about how to handle change within organisations but there appears to be a glaring gap in the applicability of this knowledge to computerisation programmes.

The non-technical dimensions of success can be grouped into three categories:

- Executive vision and leadership

- Culture and people (both senior management and staff)

- Environment: including the physical surroundings in which a business operates

Executive vision and leadership

A survey of chief executives' attitudes to IT identified two specific categories of executive. Some 75 per cent of these chief executives were concerned with internal efficiency and doing things right. The remaining 25 per cent were more concerned with looking out beyond the organisation into the market place and at their competitors. Every board will have a mixture of these inward- and outward-looking executives and, provided their influence is broadly balanced, much good can come from their perceptions of how to run the business.

Often, however, the routine of corporate activity will appear to be carved in stone to some executives, and they will then generate a degree of inertia that impedes their more innovative and imaginative fellow managers. Corporations tend to reward consistency rather than initiative and few organisations have well-recognised career ladders for those who question the status quo. Innovation must be publicly rewarded.

Apart from a reluctance to change, the other significant impediment is inexperience and a tendency to 'learn as we go'. This affects an organisation's level of technological maturity. A technologically mature organisation can be defined as one that manages the assimilation of IT into its business. Staff are at ease managing, using and experimenting with new forms of IT and there is a facility for innovating quickly and snatching competitive advantage. This definition works on the assumption that the organisation has already had some exposure to IT and that its past experience has been at least satisfactory. Change and its impact on organisations has been studied for decades. Much has been learned and much discarded. Theories of management and how they work within a framework of changes have multiplied as the complexity of business life has grown. In the past it was possible to work on the assumption that UK management was reasonably well versed in the history and theory of management and that companies were guided by a well-intentioned management cadre. A different world exists today, however; it is no longer enough for management to escort the company in its endeavours because it must now lead every single member of the organisation towards its well-defined and easily understood goal.

Effects of change

Management must be able to do more than administer the resources of the company. It should not play a passive role but rather one in which every constituent of the company is aware of its own importance and the value of other parts of the organisation. Instead of administering resources, management should be creating new resources through its own efforts.

Successful management copes with change. There are limits to how far companies, groups of people and individuals can handle rapid, unbroken periods of change. An example of how different people and technologies have different capacities for change is the 1987 stock market crash, which saw some companies panic early while others held on to their market positions or even increased their exposure as share prices plunged. On a smaller scale, companies face change within themselves and adjusting to that change can be just as difficult as coping with macro-economic events.

Set attainable goals . . .

There is much to be said for setting attainable goals, both within the company and within the industry. Frustration flows easily from failure and attempts to undertake other challenging projects will be muted if management and staff alike feel inadequate. Settling for second best and achieving it suggests that you have judged the quality of your resources correctly. However, the challenge of the single market will not tolerate under-motivation. Remember the example of Toyota, where management ordered the time taken to carry out a difficult manufacturing operation to be reduced from four hours to twelve minutes. An impossible goal that was achieved! By 1992, many impossible goals will have had to have been achieved.

and unattainable ones

Management can be aided by statements of vision, which set out in plain language how the organisation intends carrying out its business using different IT formulae. If management outlines a particular vision, end-users are then able to imagine how different techniques can be used to achieve the same goal and they can determine the context of the IT strategy. It will also help users to understand how pieces of the strategy contribute to the overall picture.

Culture and people

Corporate culture

The debate as to whether corporate culture is a constraint or a potential advantage will be re-kindled in the run-up to 1992. Some would argue that corporate culture is a constraint because it is a fixed entity that carries value for an organisation but will not accommodate strategies that do not match the culture. If it is possible to create a strong culture that breeds excellence, this suggests that the corporate culture can be changed, monitored, perhaps even managed. Those companies which exhibit an outward-looking dynamism will be better placed than insular inward-looking organisations.

Corporate culture's adaptability to change depends on a number of factors:

- The age, size and form of the organisation
- The kind of industry the organisation is in and the culture of this industry

- The degree to which the company is ready for major strategic change

- The facet of the organisation's culture that has become maladaptive

The age of a company is mirrored in its corporate culture. A young enthusiastic band of amateurs challenging convention will react to business circumstances and the opportunities of change in a different manner to a solid, respectable market leader that feels it has a responsibility to its industry in particular and society in general. Both cultures are valid as each will motivate staff, albeit in totally different ways.

Most organisations learn behaviour patterns, ways of perceiving and thinking, ways of reacting emotionally and ways of conceptualising themselves and their environment. All these can be seen as making up a corporate culture, but equally important is the set of basic assumptions which have worked well enough in the past to be considered valid and to be passed on to new members of the company. Sometimes aspects of culture may be subconscious and staff will behave in a certain way because they believe it is expected of them.

Culture auditing   A culture audit, a systematic analysis of a company's ethos, can determine whether proposed acquisitions are worth making; it can also be used in merger situations to assess where the problem areas are likely to be and the methods needed to solve these problems. It shows ways of relieving pre- and post-merger stress and how to integrate the acquisition quickly into the acquirer's own culture, operations and business. An audit will highlight:

- Formal declarations of the organisation's values

- Corporate mythology, beliefs and experience, particularly of founder heroes and leaders

- What present leaders focus on and control

- The design of physical spaces, façades and buildings

- Management development and reward mechanisms

- Systems and procedures of the organisation

- The gap between its formal and informal recruitment system

- The needs, values and expectations of recruits

- The transformation recruits are expected to go through and the degree to which they do

- How promotions and retirements are handled

- What company functions are usual and how they are organised

- How executives handle periods of stress, such as a takeover or merger

If the takeover or merger is consistent with the aims of existing human resource management activities, fine tuning of these can be attempted to help the process. The longer the period for preparation before the merger the better, while extended joint ventures provide time for the participants to develop shared standards of technical quality and performance.

Environment

The physical environment

The non-technical components of success for IT programmes extend to the physical environment in which the end-users and the systems operate. It should be given serious consideration. It is surprising how many companies will spend money on new computers yet not address the ergonomics of the work environment.

If buildings are inadequate to accommodate the changes necessary for implementing IT programmes, the success of these programmes will be affected. Some award-winning buildings erected in the UK during the 1950s have been frozen in time because they are unable to adapt to the scale of change that is now required in modern buildings. The spread of 'sick buildings' – offices in which there is an unusually high level of staff illness at any given time – is one manifestation of this problem. Another is the level of staff turnover, particularly among new recruits.

Organisations like to pride themselves on their industrial or commercial achievements and some hope that these achievements are reflected in the environment in which staff work. Quality breeds quality. Many organisations adopt a positive attitude towards art, for example, by purchasing the work of young artists. Others place an emphasis on community work, such as aiding local charities or sourcing much of their work from local suppliers.

Companies and people strive to be associated with the best. This partly explains the success of achievement schemes such as the Queen's Awards Industry and Export and the rush to scrap old corporate notepaper as soon as a company has won such an award. Internal achievement schemes generate a positive working environment, usually for very little outlay. The cost of a crystal decanter and four wine glasses plus a photograph in the in-house journal is swiftly repaid. Gentle rivalry between branches or departments can also produce dividends out of proportion to the cost of the award.

On the other hand, an environment that is wracked with scandal and headline making news from the boardroom is unlikely to be a positive influence in speeding any development programme. In some cases insider-dealing scandals have set back the ambitions of companies by years and the measures taken by management to get to the source of the illegal activity have often alienated other, loyal, members of staff.

Building design

As IT has reached further into the fabric of our working and leisure hours, the physical environment surrounding us has changed. Architecture and building design have had to meet more complex demands placed on them by IT. Floor and ceiling dimensions have altered to accommodate the miles of cabling traversing buildings; lighter, more efficient computers have affected the load-bearing characteristics of buildings and, in turn, the floor area allocated to employees. Planning densities, parking requirements and service needs/costs have led some businesses to seek to improve their information systems so that they don't need to bear the costs of having so many employees working in the office.

TWINS

Buildings themselves have become more sophisticated. Intelligent buildings can now monitor and adjust many of the functions that create an office or manufacturing environment. Costs can be contained and more efficient use of other resources permitted. One of the most sophisticated examples of intelligent buildings has been developed by NTT in Japan. Called TWINS (Towards Information Network Systems), they are two large blocks accommodating NTT's data and office activities in the Shinagawa district of Tokyo. Completed in 1986, they provide 128,000 square metres of floor-space on sixteen levels and accommodate 2,600 employees with about 8 square metres of space per person. A large area of each floor is taken up by risers: channelling dedicated either to power or to office automation. They allow for telephone cables, LANs, building control plus telephone wiring boxes, fibre optic cable termination points and LAN node control equipment. At the roof, these risers connect to antennae for satellites and subscriber radio. Building controls automatically monitor electricity and water supply, sewage, air conditioning, lifts and lighting over 16,000 control points. Extensive fire detection and security systems are also linked into the buildings' intelligence. Rainwater, and water reclaimed from cooling towers, is used to flush WCs and irrigate the landscape, while solar panels on the roof generate hot water. The heat from data-processing activities in the second building is enough to heat the two structures. Air conditioning operates in summer and winter, while in spring and autumn the motorised windows can be lowered 200 millimetres to give ventilation. There are also motorised blinds with manual back-ups. The windows are set back 600 millimetres on the north and south façades to shade them from the sun.

NTT also provides advanced telecommunications and office auto-mation services at TWINS. The telecommunications facilities include high-level telephone services, multimedia communications services, media switching services, high-speed facsimile, electronic blackboards and whiteboards, videotext, films, voice mail, facsimile mail, text mail, voice conferencing and video conferencing. As far as office automation is concerned, NTT provides services for document processing (word-processing, line diagrams, business graphics, table creation, computation); document output (clean copy compilation and output, high-speed large-volume printing); document storage, classification and retrieval; decision support (formulation of reports, simulation, decision conferencing room); scheduling control and support (scheduled activities management, conference set-up support); information management (customer information manage-ment, library materials and information management, access to exter-nal databases); routine office work (financial administration, personnel management, sales administration, electronic voucher and settlement, stock control); card-use systems (sign-in/sign-out man-agement, cafeteria operations, company credit card systems); public-oriented information (guidance on organisations, products and events, purchase order); miscellaneous information (company computer-aided education and training support, computer-aided design, software support).

Tokyo Teleport

Japan's conviction that information holds the key to its future is further illustrated by the proposed Tokyo Teleport, which it is claimed will be the first real information city. The proposed 100-hectare site in the Tokyo area is viewed as a ground base for a global satellite communications network which will act as a world information-handling centre. Businesses planned for the Teleport include financial institutions, insurance companies, software development firms and information processing companies. The Teleport, which will be linked to other Japanese centres such as Osaka and Yokohama by satellite or fibre optic cable, will import and export information and communication services. First phase investment has been estimated at £8 billion with a final development cost of almost £20 billion. An organisation's ability to manage large-scale change will be paramount, even though few organisations will be faced with tackling IT-related changes on the scale of the Tokyo Teleport. Companies planning to break into the single market should be aware of the long-term commitment and detailed planning that Japanese companies give to entering new markets. The TWINS initiative indicates just how strong the commitment is to exploiting IT.

Organisational change

One approach that has been successful in the handling of change in IT environments is that proposed by Levitt (Figure 22). This views any organisation as operating in a state of balance between four forces:

- Organisation structure
- Tasks or functions
- People
- Technology

The Levitt diamond   The essence of a Levitt diamond is that change in any single component leads to an imbalance of the forces operating elsewhere in the organisation. If an equilibrium is to be regained, change must take place in the other three parts. This illustrates why technology-focused changes alone are insufficient to improve organisational performance. The technology component cannot re-establish an organisation's balance because it is the technology that has disrupted the balance in the first place.

One of the most neglected elements in this diamond model is the task/function component. The skills of work organisation, task

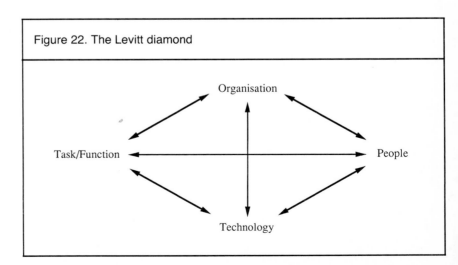

Figure 22. The Levitt diamond

restructuring, work simplification and redesign seem to be applied only rarely to IT-driven changes. Systems analysts frequently ask, 'What do you do at the moment?', rather than looking to simplify, rationalise or restructure. Technology can de-skill as well as re-skill. If management is not aware that it has this choice, technological change will almost always de-skill.

The organisation structure element of the Levitt diamond is also critical. Change as fundamental as that offered by IT must prompt discussion about current corporate structures and responsibilities. As IT orchestrates upheavals in data processing, integrated office systems, networking and telecommunications, a guiding hand becomes necessary to determine priorities between the individual areas. IT's ability to affect key business processes, such as opening up new channels of distribution, or performing as a competitive weapon, has forced boardroom attention to it.

The people component of the diamond is perhaps one of the most important non-technical factors involved in the IT analysis, and in many ways the least understood and analysed. People need to be prepared for major changes, and supported through training as new skills are acquired. Uncertainty can rapidly lead to resistance to change which can delay the take-up of information systems. Attention has, therefore, to be paid to the people factors in change situations.

The process of change

Change in an organisation will be brought about by a wide spectrum of people from the shop floor to the boardroom. This is the process of change and it depends on leadership and the ability to sell the benefits of the change to the rest of the organisation. This experience has been compressed into a simple yet powerful model (Figure 23). The essence of the model is that at every stage there is an initial period of 'opening up' – looking for information, considering alternatives, examining competitors – followed by a period of focusing on critical relationships, inter-dependencies and putting forward hypotheses to be tested at later stages. By moving ahead in a series of discrete steps (and moving back when necessary) it is possible to advance the organisation progressively. Critical decisions need to be taken before progressing from one step to another.

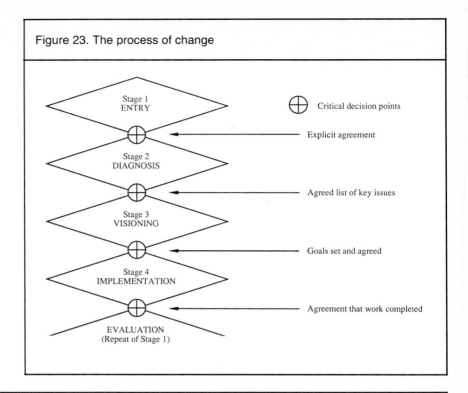

Figure 23. The process of change

The four stages of change

- The entry stage can arise out of technology problems or issues

- The diagnosis stage includes all aspects of the Levitt diamond – technology, tasks/functions, people and organisational structure

- The visioning stage will be based on a clear understanding of the current situation and will provide an IT infrastructure capable of delivering the goals

- Implementation will follow provided the diagnosis and visioning have indicated sufficiently high returns on investment

Senior management commitment

Senior management must display a commitment, not only to the technology, but to the specific business gains they expect from IT. Management must, in addition, have a complete understanding of the changes that will be necessary in the organisation if these benefits are to be achieved.

Although corporate strategies exist and strategic intent is recognisable at senior level, many companies do not have a concise, coherent and comprehensive plan that guides the entire organisation. All too often the planning is biased towards the technical component, and the human and work organisational aspects are neglected. Organisational structure also frequently adds to the problems rather than providing a vehicle for developing appropriate solutions. This must change if companies are to be in a position to exploit the single market opportunities.

The quality of management

Management must communicate effectively

While most companies maintain they have an IT strategy, only a minority have it formally documented as part of an overall business strategy. Over three-quarters of UK companies have reservations about the success of their IT strategy. This appears to be a case of management inability to communicate some of the simpler elements of its activities. Fortunately for the UK, it is not alone in this.

The gap between expectation and realised gains was illustrated in a recent survey of 700 US companies. The systems executives in 77 per cent of these companies felt their systems department was performing its job well while only 57 per cent of the CEOs felt that their systems departments were meeting the needs of the company. Over three-quarters of the systems executives believed they were helping to set the course of the company, while only 63 per cent of the CEOs agreed. Significantly, only 50 per cent of the CEOs felt computers cut costs, compared with 70 per cent of the systems executives.

One of the clear lessons from this survey is that systems departments should focus more on cutting costs and on communicating to senior management how much they have saved the company. Communication within an organisation will not happen by itself.

Managerial perceptions of IT have a profound impact on the effectiveness of computer projects. It is obvious that the involvement of senior management is crucial and the most successful strategies are those which involve management on a regular basis from the initial preparation of the strategy. Failure stems from managers who remain aloof, remote and who have a poor understanding of, or no respect for, computers.

Duality of vision

Breakout potential

Depending on the perception that is dominant within an organisation, IT can provide either an inward or outward breakout potential. Looking within the organisation, IT addresses operational effectiveness, administrative efficiency, organisational change and human relations. The external breakout vision sees the chance of dealing with the effectiveness of the company in terms of its customers, suppliers and competitors. The two approaches are not mutually exclusive – the mature company looks in both directions. To derive maximum benefit from the dual view, a company needs to handle its IT skilfully so that it can support both the internal administrative functions, and the monitoring of market and competitor activity.

The need for a paradigm shift

As more organisations seek new ways to gain competitive advantage over rivals, it becomes increasingly difficult to find ways of achieving this competitive edge. Any advantage will prove to be short lived. Something extra will have to be found to give organisations a better grip on their markets and to ward off competition.

In the physical sciences, the notion that a paradigm shift takes place every few hundred years is widely accepted. Things which were taken for granted are questioned, a new way of looking at the world emerges. Copernicus and Galileo were responsible for the paradigm shift that allowed us to view the sun, not the earth, as the centre of our immediate place in space. IT is looking for a change in outlook as fundamental as this.

The new paradigm must embrace more than the technology push, and the Levitt diamond indicates some other vital components to organisational change. Even within the technology component there needs to be a fundamental shift towards a greater concern with integrating the various technology sub-systems. There are few 'greenfield' sites so far as technology within organisations are concerned. The emphasis has to be on how to move from the current state of affairs to a more integrated situation, where the outputs of one system become the inputs for the next system. Other elements of the required new paradigm relate to the ways in which the organisation targets, measures, and realises the benefits from an IT investment.

The benefits/beneficiary matrix (Figure 24) has the advantage of focusing both internally and externally in a systematic way. Much recent debate has concentrated on the potential for external customer links and neglected internal efficiency, effectiveness and added value. There is a danger an organisation will price itself out of a market or not deliver the appropriate goods or services. However, by being efficient and effective an organisation can create barriers to its rivals. The matrix does not neglect customer orientation, which is so important in getting the right goods and services to the customer. And this balance between internal and external factors is another important ingredient of the new paradigm.

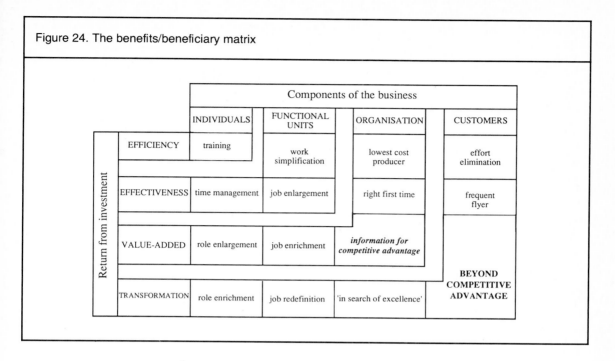

Figure 24. The benefits/beneficiary matrix

The new paradigm will take the organisation beyond a concern with piecemeal application and opportunities for individual and limited competitive opportunities. A 'Big Bang' approach is not necessary. Instead each organisation in the future will have some fundamental questions to ask, and answer, about the nature of its IT. Will it be proprietary? Will it be piecemeal? Will there be rigid limits to it? Will it allow evolution?

The core of the new paradigm is a concern with balance:

- Balance between generation of information and the use of that information

- Balance between various components of an organisation

- Balance between internal and external outlooks

With an executive push and continuous support, UK organisations could exploit the single market opportunities with a firm foundation of information and IT.

Like a painter's fresh canvas, this is a real challenge which should not be cluttered with a backlog of existing work or problems. Freed from the reality of how the company operates, there is the time for vision and boldness of execution. In this new start the first brush strokes will prove crucial to the final image.

The corporate culture in which the management operates will be partly reflected in the managers' approach to their blank canvas. Establishing a creative culture will be absolutely necessary if the company is to adapt to the depth and scale of upheaval that 1992 promises. As the CEO and senior management stand in front of their blank canvas, they will be faced with setting themselves goals that may be considered realistic or unrealistic. If the organisation has no tradition of coping with change, it will have to learn quickly.

III
Making IT happen in Europe

9. Establishing the European IT organisation

Technology can help minimise cultural differences

Today few truly European-wide companies exist, partly because they are inherently difficult to establish and operate and partly because there has been no need for them in the past. Corporate archives are peppered with case studies of failed trans-national mergers in Europe. The most notable successes have been with UK and Dutch companies – Unilever and Royal Dutch/Shell – but these are exceptions and not recent. As a rule, trans-national mergers have not worked in Europe.

Although the EC may be a relatively small geographic area, the low level of economic and business integration has meant that the real boundaries are intangible: culture, language, nationalism, education, politics, and a host of other factors that makes each European country distinct from another. International expansion, even if you know the language and think you know the business, can be even more difficult, as Midland Bank's costly foray into the Californian retail banking market shows.

Information systems have never been restricted by geographic boundaries. Instead they have aided the growth of multinational organisations by providing a technical infrastructure to smooth over the constraints of time and distance. Time and distance are not major obstacles for the bulk of the Community since most of the manufacturing industry is concentrated within a two-hour time zone with a diameter of perhaps 1,000 miles. The physical and temporal boundaries of the EC are quite small if compared with the USA and minuscule if compared with the Soviet Union.

The IT companies themselves have made the greatest progress towards truly multinational status. They have managed to leap-frog national and cultural barriers by applying in an imaginative way the very technology they are selling to their customers. In the process of building pan-European (or pan-Continental) corporations, IT companies have created a base from which to expand into intercontinental or global businesses. Olivetti was a European business information company before it became a global enterprise, and the same can be said of IBM in North and South America. Digital and Hewlett-Packard have perhaps gone furthest in establishing a global culture, and both make extensive use of IT to preserve and evolve that culture.

Communications

With the liberalisation of data and information flows across national borders after 1992, there will exist for the first time in the EC the chance for companies to run themselves as European multinationals instead of single-country nationals with foreign subsidiaries. This transition can be supported through IT, but not without re-appraising the current role of IT in a company. The IT world is changing rapidly and the basic components of an IT infrastructure have grown in power and sophistication. This means looking at how the technology should operate in the organisation and who should have responsibility for it.

IT can straddle boundaries

It is widely agreed that competition within the EC will increase dramatically as some of the more obvious barriers to commerce are removed. IT will be at the forefront of achieving competitive advantage in this environment and promises to be able to straddle, but not necessarily break down, the boundaries of culture and language. Management will have to recognise that the business and information strategies that were used to develop a market position in the UK will not necessarily advance the company's activities in a post-1992 Europe. Now is the time to reposition the company's strategy and to establish priorities and revise schedules.

Merging IT infrastructures

A search for business alliances, partners or acquisitions will be part of this realignment. The speed at which merged companies can function as a single unit and how long it takes a takeover target to be fully digested will depend on the state of their IT infrastructures. Totally incompatible information systems will hinder the smooth evolution of a business. IT managers will be forced to impose order on a chaotic jumble of screens, keyboards, minicomputers and perhaps even mainframes. Entire systems may have to be thrown out – and there is no guarantee that the redundant IT system will be that of the smaller foreign acquisition.

IT will become a key component in the drive for greater European market share. Good, flexible and responsive systems will become the cornerstone of the organisation's success. The company will need to pick the winning projects and focus the development effort of the information systems on them, while maintaining and updating existing systems that run the organisation.

Overcoming cultural boundaries

Companies that begin to internationalise will find they need senior managers with international management experience and awareness. Such new needs will affect recruitment criteria and development policies. The growth in joint ventures and acquisitions and mergers will also have an impact on the way companies need to manage their staff.

Mergers and acquisitions activities create tension, block promotions, generate conflicts of loyalty, fuel compensation gaps and cause exile syndromes, communications blockages, rumour mills, personal uncertainty, resistance to change, culture shock and high staff turnover. Longer-term problems may arise out of the integration of corporate cultures, staff transfers and the restructuring of the organisation and its policies. Overcoming these problems will be an important part of the single market strategy.

Foster an international culture

Companies will have to foster an international culture. Recent research indicates that the real barriers to export activities are largely internal and behavioural and, therefore, need a conscious effort on the part of the company to break them down. Elements of a human resource strategy that encourage an international culture include:

- High rewards for managers who get involved in international activities

- Hiring internationally experienced middle and senior managers and promoting on such experience

- Operating incentive programmes linked to international activities and incorporating this into performance appraisals

Human resource management

Human resource management can create real strategic advantages in a number of ways. Companies can plan manpower needs or succession activities to link personnel programmes to suit the corporate strategy. Thus, if the company has embarked on a three- or five-year programme, it will need to match its staffing policy to the programme's timescale, rather than hiring freelances or short-contract staff. It must also identify the human resource strengths of the company and gear business strategies towards gaining a competitive advantage with these. A company bulging with fluent French speakers would hardly be using its staff profitability if it concentrated on German-speaking markets.

Another approach is to use coherent employment policies that are underpinned by a 'people philosophy'. Digital, for example, has a no-redundancy policy which the company adhered to during the most recent computer industry recession in the mid-1980s. IBM has also had until recently a full employment policy that had a profound effect on the way it operated. An IBM executive described the situation as 'having people for life. You have to train and retrain them, make sure you have enough staff, but not too many staff for the long term. Individuals realise that they are in the company for good and have to make the most of it. It becomes the individual's responsibility to optimise his or her own performance and value to the company.'

Labour mobility

Companies are simply combinations of people helping to make money. No profit will exist in a wide open European market if a company does not have the right calibre of staff in the right location. Labour mobility, assumed by many to be one of the key gains of the unified market, will be concentrated in the well-qualified classes and will not filter through generally until much later. Job losses, rather than gains, are expected initially. Paolo Cecchini in *1992: The European Challenge* predicts a 'J-curve in employment with an initial loss of 225,000 jobs offset later by a net increase of two to five million jobs over time'. Stockbrokers James Capel suggest that if there are any skill shortages, they will be for qualified engineers.

Demographics

The UK also faces a demographic time bomb itself. The number of 16- to 24-year-olds in the labour force is forecast to plunge by the mid-1990s and available youth employment (broadly young people in their first and second jobs) is set to fall by 1.2 million (or one-fifth). This shortfall will need to be made up by employing higher numbers of women (aged 25 to 44) and by increasing the use of part-time labour.

Managing human resources

Human resource management is associated with the handling of many aspects of the people that make up an organisation. All companies include people with different levels of skill, backgrounds, expectations and abilities. It is up to the management to derive the maximum benefit from these people for the good of the company. Management must motivate itself, and then motivate the rest of the workforce. It must look at the whole spectrum of employment – from recruitment to retirement.

Recruitment and skill supply

Tight labour markets at local, industry, or national levels have created a need to tap new supplies of labour while regional differences in pay

Shortage of skilled labour

levels and the cost of living have decreased labour mobility. In the Community, the freedom of labour movement will be one of the great long-term achievements of the single market. But it will not occur overnight and it will be confined, at first, to the well-educated and the specialist, and only later will it filter through to the less skilled workforce. The shortage of skilled people in the Community as we approach 1992 will be partially overcome by companies looking beyond the EC and into EFTA countries and the USA for highly trained and experienced personnel.

New blood

Bringing in new blood is an essential feature of cultural change. The scale of new product development that the single European market will trigger will place an enormous burden on the skills and abilities of existing staff in many companies, and companies may find it necessary to enter completely new labour markets to find the necessary skills. Headhunting of people with the right marketing and product experience is already accelerating.

Recruitment programmes

To secure a steady supply of good workers, companies will look more often than previously at recruitment from colleges and secondary schools, not only in the UK but in the Community at large. Companies that halted recruitment programmes in the early 1980s as a reaction to the economic recession will find themselves particularly vulnerable to staff shortages at senior levels. Such development gaps within a company's ranks will prove difficult to fill. Some financial institutions are already suffering the consequences of this freezing of the corporate headcount.

A major management tool has been the manipulation of recruitment criteria. Some companies have raised recruitment standards to develop a more flexible skill base. This has the effect of challenging some other aspects of the human resources system such as career opportunities and training, management style and employment conditions. Other companies have widened the net and increased the volume of recruits, which places pressure on training to bridge the gap between entry standards and required job skills.

Training and retraining

Staff are already expensive to find, place and develop. After 1992, they will be even more expensive and subject to a greater degree of poaching. A systematic training programme and a reputation as a company that provides good training will entice many young hopefuls to an organisation. If the management approach is well-defined and considered, most staff will repay this training with loyalty, at least for a number of years. Retraining, particularly for companies that tend to

Job simulation

employ people for their entire working lives, will grow in importance as the EC markets undergo successive upheavals in the next ten years.

IT has many roles to play in training and retraining exercises, and the more innovative companies that are prepared to experiment with job simulation – where a trainee mimics the working activities of his tutor on screen – will derive higher returns than those with a Dickensian approach to indentures or apprenticeship. Even in industries that use cheap part-time labour, there is a need for a stable and informed workforce, and efforts have been made to reduce and control attrition. One managing director summed up the issue: 'If firms are losing people as soon as they have trained them, they have got their training right and everything else wrong.'

Changing work patterns

Flexible employment contracts

Increased time flexibility and a greater reliance on part-time labour are two important aspects of work systems that could help companies cope with the forthcoming changes. Flexible employment contracts within a company are important if work patterns are to be adapted to the needs of the company and the skills of the individual. These will grow in importance as the demand for skilled labour increases after 1992.

Maintain continuity of training

Skill structures have been radically changed as job definitions have become integrated, fused, or blurred. Some companies have been forced to develop a cross-functional integration of IT and customer relation skills as a way to gain competitive strategies. In addition to looking at the ways a company can influence its human resource management, it is worth examining the reasons why companies start and stop training and what can be done to maintain a continuity in training. The most often cited trigger for training is technical change or product-market developments that lead to a perceived 'skill gap'. The greater the level of change the organisation sustains, the greater the impact of training will be. The installation of a completely automated material handling process, for example, will affect front-line production workers and have a knock-on effect on maintenance staff, production management and production engineers.

Major capital investment without an accompanying investment in training courts the risk of corporate failure. It is easy to incorporate training as part of a capital expense when new wide-ranging systems are involved. A greater awareness that a company's future prosperity is linked to the quality of its personnel and their skills, as is understood by the computer software industry, can prevent short-cuts in training programmes. Many companies, however, still feel that training is a tap that can be turned on and off and that after the successful implementation of a major programme, there is no longer a need to sustain a large training effort. Such attitudes thrive where there is no training culture, which forms part of the larger corporate culture.

Some organisations have an open career structure but place little value on formal learning. The absence of a 'qualifications culture' may be the result of a growth era that encouraged promotion to management positions of people lacking formal qualifications. Rapid promotion may be the best way to deal with short-term corporate emergencies, but the failure to review staff qualifications and upgrade personnel training is a recipe for long-term under-performance for the company and employee alike. Companies that focus training on clerical and technical skills and exclude proper management training run the risk of distorting the effectiveness of the entire organisation. The impetus for promoting training and ensuring its continuity must be provided by senior management.

Differing work ethics

When UK organisations start to recruit from Continental Europe they will need to be aware of the differences in national work ethics. Staff in the UK are enticed by higher salaries and highly creative environments, whereas German or Austrian workers may seek clearly defined job roles. Scandinavian employees may tend to innovate more than their central European counterparts, but they also place a high value on the organisation's concern for people and the quality of life. French, Belgian and Italian staff tend not to accept delegated power as readily as the British. Regardless of what types of national characteristics may exist, it is important for management to accept that it may be impossible to implement a uniform strategy across Europe.

Teleworking will increase

Remote working

Companies will need to adopt creative employment strategies if they are to keep prized members of staff. Innovative employment models such as 'remote' working (working from home) have grown in importance. The three best documented examples in the computer industry are ICL's CPS Programming Services, Rank Xerox's networking experiment and F International's use of home-based freelances. It is important to realise that each model has major differences: the ICL staff are pensionable employees of the company, while Xerox relies on self-employed people running separate businesses and F International uses only contract staff.

A close look at the ICL experience shows the advantages and disadvantages of remote working. ICL started the scheme in 1968 and extended it rapidly in the 1980s principally to retain female technical authors who were leaving to have children. ICL was thus able to retain existing employees who had a commitment to the company; it still achieved a return on its training investment and retained skilled jobs. Knowledge of the company systems was retained by the staff allowing for easy transfer across sites; the staff were cheaper than freelances and were more popular with remaining on-site staff. The company found, however, that its overhead costs were still high on account of National Insurance, sickness and maternity leave obligations. It had an obligation to find work for the staff, and found that more management time was necessary for staff development and there was a danger of having to pay for unproductive time.

The language problem

A survey by IDS has warned of the dangers of underestimating the language problem. There are thousands of people in the professional and managerial classes in other European countries with three or more languages, but relatively few in the UK. Marketing and distribution sectors, however, require a local presence and an ability to speak the local language will be vital. The survey concludes that 'multi-lingual executives are going to be at a premium in Britain'. At the moment the shortage of language teachers may be endangering UK preparations for 1992. Stock market analysts Kleinwort Grieveson take it further. 'UK companies may have to pay more of a premium to acquire staff with language skills and cultural familiarity with continental countries. The ability to work across national frontiers may be more a matter of attitude of mind than a matter of skill.'

Human resources management – the challenge

A recent survey into UK corporate attitudes towards human resource development in IT produced startling evidence that the UK faces an enormous task in changing outdated management practices if it is to gain the maximum from its highly skilled workforce:

- 86 per cent of the IT departments covered in the survey had been reorganised in the past two years, and 54 per cent within the last year. There is a move to integrate IT departments more fully into the business structure.

- Few IT departments have developed a coherent personnel retention strategy.

- 82 per cent felt that retaining would help overcome skills obsolescence.

- Training tends to be focused on technical aspects of jobs.

- IT departments need to develop their skills in management, which the survey concluded were poor.

- Less than one-third of IT departments had board representation; only 48 per cent of the companies attempt to plan formally the careers of IT staff.

- 54 per cent of IT departments plan their human resources one year ahead and 25 per cent take a two-year (or longer) strategic view.

Towards the European information systems department

The fundamental debate that surrounds information systems (IS) departmental structures concerns their scale and optimum size. A large IS department may be preserved, even promoted, in the hope of attracting rare skills that can then be developed and retained. This is backed up by a perception of the need of common facilities across the units. At the other end of the scale will be the individual unit that approaches IS on a market-oriented basis and requires the department to treat business units as customers and achieves its funding from the sales revenue its services attract.

Five main categories of IS department have been identified and each has its own particular benefits:

- Centralised: A unified function that reports to the corporate management. Distributed equipment may exist but it is under the operational control of the central IS.

- Business unit: Another unified function but run this time as a business within the organisation and reports in the same way as other business units. Its business activity is largely or wholly with other business units in the group and it charges for its services, although there is no obligation for these units to use the IS service.

- Business venture: Similar to the IS business unit but with a clear aim of generating revenue for itself and the group as a whole by selling products and services inside and outside the organisation. Signs of this type of operation are dedicated external salesmen, marketing literature, published tariffs, revenue targets and some products that are not available to the internal organisation.

- Decentralised: IS is a distributed function. Each business unit contains its own IS capability under its own control. There is no central IS responsibility except for the support of corporate headquarters functions. The unit's capital and budget submissions are reviewed by central management under general financial planning and control procedures.

- Federal: Again IS is a distributed function with each business unit containing and controlling its own IS capability. There is, in addition, a central IS unit reporting to the corporate management which has responsibility for defined aspects of policy and architecture across the organisations and which may deliver some common or shared services.

Regardless of the category into which the system falls, the IS director has a number of key responsibilities:

- Understanding the business processes
- Creating a vision for the future and selling it
- Establishing the systems department's credibility
- Helping others feel comfortable with the technology
- Implementing a systems architecture
- Ensuring quality is implemented

Two important variables exist that will guide the evolution of the IS structure. The first is that IS arrangements should align with key characteristics of the host organisations and the second that IS cannot be expected to operate successfully unless it conforms to the basic structure and management style of the organisation it serves. Furthermore, the culture and history of IS management must not be ignored. The IS architect must be sensitive to what works and what does not, since any measure of abrupt change will induce a loss of momentum and disrupt the effectiveness of the business.

As IS structures evolve, the question will arise as to who is in control and who is responsible for what. To achieve this balance between end-users and specialists, the following model has been proposed:

- If the strategic impact of future applications is assessed as low, and the technology required is mature, efficiency becomes paramount and IS specialists should be given the responsibility of achieving it.

- If the strategic impact is low but new technology is required – i.e. risk is high compared with potential business benefits – the desirability of proceeding with the project should be questioned.

- When relatively mature technology is coupled with perceptions of high strategic importance, the end-users should be in control of the IS strategy but the specialists should be charged with control of the implementation. Devolution to the business of some development resource may be important while devolution of operations will not.

- When a high strategic impact is combined with immature technology, the entire activity should be positioned within the user function with an unabashed emphasis on 'effectiveness'.

Research in Scandinavia on high-growth companies suggests that the absence of a formal organisational structure will encourage disproportionate business achievements. High-growth companies are traditionally medium-sized organisations that hold a market or product dominance. Instead of operating in formal hierarchical structures, the staff in many high-growth companies form teams that assemble and dissolve depending on the circumstances. With few formal procedures, control mechanisms are kept to a minimum and innovators are not only allowed to innovate but encouraged to do so.

Creating the IT supremo

Increasing sophistication in hardware, software and the applicability of computers has meant that the traditional data processing manager's perspective has changed. Data processing had the effect of centralising information while the modern IT function aims to decentralise the information by making it available throughout the company. User attitudes have also changed. Fear of technology is on the decline and management is beginning to understand what IT-based systems can do for them and what they are doing for their competitors.

IT supremo's tasks   Competitive pressures have turned modern business life into an unforgiving battleground as markets are internationalised and customers expect a better service, a choice of supplier and more frequent choice of new products. To survive in this environment, IT must be used strategically. Suppliers and customers must be linked more closely and barriers must be built against competitors, new market entrants and substitute products. A clever IT strategy may actually change the basic economics of the business. These are the tasks of the IT supremo. The basic building block today in creating a more positive environment for the entire IT strategy is to have someone responsible for all aspects of IT within a company. Such a business systems director will operate at board level with the same degree of authority as other directors.

But before any giant leap forward is taken, the IT supremo must be meeting the company's expectations. The IT supremo must provide the right technical architecture, with sufficient processing power, and an infrastructure of hardware and software on which systems that support the business can be built. He or she must be able to cope with key issues of quality, responsiveness, reliability of service at an acceptable price and value for money.

Return on investment

The organisation must get a decent return on its investment, but it is crucial for the IT supremo to allow progress to be measured by parameters that are capable of quantifying IT gains. The supremo must also manage corporate expectations. Lack of middle and top management support for IT is one of the most commonly cited reasons for lack of success in IT projects. It is not surprising that boardroom unease develops when some IT expenditure grows at rates of 30 to 40 per cent per annum.

Since IT can play a vital role in gaining and holding competitive advantage in a single market, the IT supremo must show how the company will be disadvantaged if the competition uses IT strategically and the company does not. Management must also be made aware of existing uses of IT in its own market and must decide whether the company has the correct technology base on which to build strategic systems. The organisation must supply the right balance of direct and indirect resources to build Euro-organisations. It is up to the IT supremo to be able to specify what the correct mix will be and follow the strategy through.

Corporate vision

Management must provide vision. The board, as a group, or the chief executive, as an individual, must know what is sought from IT. Corporate visions abound and they are as diverse as the companies they come from:

- The head of a retail toy store chain summarised his vision of inventory control: 'As a customer purchases an item off the shelf, I want an invisible hand to replace it.'

- An insurance company chief executive's objective was that all customers telephoning the company would be able to do their business with a single call.

- British Telecom hopes to create 'one front office' in each area through which all customer enquiries and contacts will be handled. Each unit would be responsible for customer satisfaction in its own area.

- Some local authorities hope to establish single local offices that offer the general public access to various housing, public health and leisure services.

A step-by-step approach

The strategy for success is built on individual steps and a blind rush forward leads nowhere. The steps are:

1. Recognise that 1992 represents a real opportunity for the company and for human resource and information systems in particular.

2. Look at the 1992 opportunity with fresh eyes rather than in terms of existing or past strategies. Be prepared to review and revise strategies.

3. Begin to think at least on a European scale. Europe may be the springboard to global trading.

4. Manage information and people as a strategic resource and ensure there are the right systems to support the most critical portions of the company.

5. Place greater emphasis on the process associated with large-scale change and do not ignore non-technical issues.

6. Give people-management and innovative skills the recognition they deserve.

7. Reward the IT cadre with financial and promotional inducements. If you fail to do so, competitors will headhunt them.

The single market is yet another in the long line of challenges facing human resource and information managers. It is within the scope of the IT function of companies to exploit the new opportunities and generate sustainable business advantage. The human resource professionals have an important role in providing the framework within which this can happen.

10. Managing European projects

A company's success after 1992 will depend largely on its ability to implement successfully a range of large and small IT projects before (and after) the single market comes into existence. This means that companies have less than three years to identify, approve and implement major projects. The quality of approach to project management will, therefore, be vital if these companies are to succeed.

Modern project management began with the Manhattan Project, which developed the atomic bomb during the Second World War. US military work in the 1950s on intercontinental ballistic missile systems expanded the knowledge base for handling large-scale project management while NASA's lunar landing programme in the 1960s extended the work further. The successes achieved on these projects have not been repeated on IT projects, which all too often run late, overspend, and do not deliver the needed solution. It is clear, therefore, that the lessons of defence and aerospace projects are not being transferred successfully to the commercial IT arena.

Too many IT failures

Peter W. G. Morris, executive director of the Major Projects Association, suggests that IT's mixed success has two basic causes:

- Project management approaches and disciplines often fail to satisfy the basic criteria for success

- IT projects, because of the intangible nature of the deliverables, are more difficult to implement

In a major US study of project management effectiveness, Morris collected a vast amount of data on nearly 1,500 company projects. This revealed that the final costs matched the initial estimates in only thirty or so cases.

If project management's concern is to implement a development on time, within budget and to technical specification, then serious deficiencies exist. The striking discovery Morris made was that the factors that prevented the project staying within budget were often of a strategic nature, or were external to the project: government actions, inflation, strikes, technical uncertainty, quantity order changes, scope changes and the weather. Project management, Morris concluded, had to start facing up to the strategic and external factors that were so clearly compromising its ability to perform. Some of the conditions for success are considered at the end of this chapter.

Projects exist to deliver benefits

Executive direction and commitment

All too often the enthusiasm of the project team clouds and distorts the basic purpose of the exercise. Companies have to be totally committed to the concept of the business-driven project with overall leadership coming from a senior business manager, who ensures that the emphasis on the business needs and the required benefits does not slip. The corollary to this is that European-scale IT projects will need to be handled carefully if success is to be achieved within the relatively short timespan available. Furthermore there will be a need to be flexible in the approach to 1992 projects. Not every project will be a key strategic initiative on which the fate of the organisation hangs. Many will be quick, dirty and cheap – but necessary. Some tactical IT projects might require only meagre resources and a project champion. However, both categories of project require the same degree of management expertise and commitment from the top.

Successful management of projects to prepare for 1992 will, therefore, involve four stages:

1. Creating the management environment, which should include a definition of the project

2. Managing the project risks proactively

3. Establishing and agreeing the plans and control techniques

4. Implementing the tools (usually computerised) to support the techniques

The plans, control techniques, and tools will not differ greatly from normal complex projects. But the organisational issues associated with setting up an adequate management environment will be much more complex and difficult to operate effectively, and the risks identified by Morris's research will be much more real.

The risks will develop from the additional demands of the pan-European projects which arise out of the establishment of the single market, namely:

- Multiple physical locations

- Differing national management cultures

- Languages, both within the project and perhaps for the end-user, documentation and training

- Differing requirements of the system for different countries arising from different business pressures, different local customs and different regulations (even after 1992)

- Most importantly, uncertainty about how the regulatory issues facing the single market will be resolved

Thus to achieve success in the single market it will be necessary to concentrate mainly on the issues involved in creating an effective management environment, including realistic risk management.

Key management environment issues

There are a variety of issues to be addressed in setting up an effective management environment, of which the most important are:

- Organisation structure: Companies will need to examine how multiple users in multiple countries agree on requirements; how the skills of different functions in different countries are used; how management will be exercised given the three elements of project responsibility, functional responsibility and country responsibility.

- Roles and responsibilities: The roles and responsibilities of the various parties will need to be clarified and enforced. Functional or national barons cannot be tolerated and significant initial planning will be needed to resist these tendencies.

- Lines of communication: Effective communication will need to be achieved. While physical proximity is always desirable in a project team, the likely distance between elements of the team dealing with different countries may render this impossible. More effort than normal must be allowed for and then devoted to communication.

- Authority levels and decision making: An effective decision-making apparatus will need to be established and pan-European authority must be given to decision makers.

- Business objectives and scope of work: Despite the single market, there will remain different practices and different cultures within the different countries. Companies will, therefore, have different business needs, products, customers, marketing strategies, and delivery systems, all of which will need to be catered for within the 1992 project. The utmost effort will be needed to avoid a degeneration into a series of single country projects, thereby losing the pan-EC benefits.

- Standards: The single market will create many common standards, but 1992 projects will need to be carried out prior to 1992. The introduction and phasing in of common standards will need to be carefully monitored.

Structured Project Management

Even without a multi-country dimension more projects fail because of organisational problems and management environment problems than for any other cause. An extension of the Structured Project Management approach is advisable. This has been used successfully on large complex IT projects (often involving several countries) over the last ten years. It essentially involves creating a management environment based on:

- Developing a project culture and organisation.

- Imposing discipline (people must do the same things in the same way).

- Creating visibility (control and information systems must be clear and standard throughout the project).

- Using the right people (knowledge and experience cannot easily be acquired on the project. It becomes imperative that the best and most experienced people in the organisation, or from the outside, are used).

That is: reducing risk through good management practice. This method entails the use of a management plan to help create and maintain the management environment. This is a simple device but, if used properly, it will resolve conflicts and confusion before the project starts and throughout its duration. It will be the mechanism for drawing disagreements and misunderstandings out into the open for resolution early in the life of the project. It must be formally agreed so that all parties are committed to it. Once it is agreed, it forms a solid foundation upon which the management environment can be built and effective management can be based.

The management plan

As we have already stated, the overriding purpose of all projects is to generate benefit for the business. A project, therefore, comprises three phases:

- Agreement of the business needs

- Construction of a product

- Use of the product to generate benefits for the organisation

Unfortunately, far too many projects focus upon the construction phase at the expense of the business needs and benefits. Decisions are taken by a narrowly focused, often technical, team. However, for the project to be business driven all three parts must be thought through before construction starts; this is a key function of the management plan. Attention must be paid to defining the business needs in a clear way so that requirements do not fluctuate. The question of how the benefits will be delivered must be addressed as early as possible; it cannot be neglected until the product is virtually complete.

For 1992 projects the business needs will be difficult to define, and a clear approach to releasing the benefit will be more difficult to identify, since a variety of parties with differing needs and aspirations will be involved. The question of how the various parties can be drawn together to define a common need, and to co-operate on delivering maximum benefit, is of fundamental importance to the successful conclusion of all 1992 projects. Projects must be managed with the three key elements mentioned above clearly in mind. It is equally important to recognise that no project can be considered in isolation. Most organisations will be carrying out a number of multi-country projects at any time, together with their usual quota of normal projects.

In preparing for 1992 projects, an organisation can quickly identify a wide range of opportunities. These will include presenting a unified public image, merger with or acquisition of other companies, growth through technology, enhanced R&D effectiveness enabling a sharper market focus to be achieved. Responses to these opportunities may range from product innovation and internal organisational co-operation to a concentration on core activities. These responses will take the form of strategic programmes in corporate repositioning, a co-ordination of research, development of managerial potential and the fostering of standards of excellence throughout the organisation. These in turn will generate demands for systems to support marketing, finance, sales and administration. Structures and mechanisms are needed to review, evaluate, authorise, prioritise, and then manage the entire programme of projects as an integrated whole, against the background of clear business and IT strategies. Unless all these issues are thoroughly examined at the outset, agreed between the parties, and documented in the management plan, then success will be elusive.

So the management plan must cover a number of areas; particularly:

- Definition of business needs
- An outline of the scope of work
- Projected benefits
- Organisation of the project
- Roles and responsibilities
- Lines of communication
- Authority levels
- Outline of control mechanisms
- Outline of how the benefit will be generated

Focus on key projects

Project prioritisation will become a critical area in the run-up to 1992. Not every project can be undertaken and when more than one is considered, the inter-dependencies of the projects must be considered.

If each of these points is tackled rigorously at the outset, resolved, and this gains widespread management commitment, risks are reduced and the probability of success is increased.

Implementing the management plan

However, the management plan is just the starting point. It will take effort, resources, and difficult decisions to put the plan into effect. There is a wide range of areas to be tackled, but some of the most critical elements of implementation are:

- Experienced, forceful project managers with adequate time and authority to tackle the work.

- Clear mechanisms for cutting across, and for resolving inter-country problems and disagreements. One person must be given the authority to say yes or no.

- The centre must concentrate on defining how the project fits with the business strategy, what the requirements are, what its priority is, and what are the key targets for each work area.

- Work areas must be clearly allocated to each country, with clear targets. Then the country must be given responsibility to manage – do not try to manage everything from the centre.

- Heavy emphasis must be placed on adequate control techniques, skills and systems. The centre must know what is planned and what is taking place throughout the project, otherwise it will fall apart. So the centre will define standardised control techniques and systems to be adopted by all work areas.

Each work area will plan and control its own work against agreed targets. Plans and progress reports will be consolidated so that the centre can develop master plans and master reports. It is then possible to direct the whole project and to solve project-wide problems.

Nevertheless, once established the management plan must not be regarded as fixed and unchanging. It will need to be re-examined at regular intervals and kept up to date otherwise it will lose its impact. But, if the management plan is maintained as a clear and well understood project charter, it will allow every decision to be taken in context, and a project that can take decisions quickly and effectively is well on the way to success.

Establishing the project control system

The successful implementation of 1992 projects will not be achieved by inventing new methods and new systems for management and control. It will be achieved by doing basic things well and also by recognising the additional complexity which the multi-country organisational issues will present. Those projects which recognise the organisational problems, and resolve them at an early point by preparing and agreeing an effective management plan, will be the ones that lead the way.

Implementation framework

The management plan will set out the approved framework for implementing the project. It will set targets, outline the implementation approach and define responsibilities. Project controls must then be set up to ensure the project is implemented according to the plan.

The control cycle

To be effective, project controls must draw managers' attention to critical areas and forthcoming problems. Managers must then exercise control by taking positive action to correct deviations. The process is illustrated by the control cycle (Figure 25), the elements of which and the key points relating to each element are outlined below.

Original plan	Define deliverables
	Allocate responsibilities
	Identify resources
	Estimate costs
	Estimate timescales
Review progress	Measure real achievement, not effort
	Estimate work to be done, time it will take to complete and resources/cost to complete
	Compare with the plan, identify variances
	Be realistic
	Monitor quality

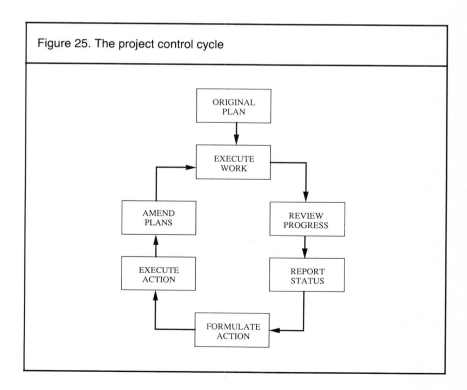

Figure 25. The project control cycle

Report status	Give *true* situation
	Be clear and comprehensive
	Indicate variance from the plan
	Report exceptions
	Indicate trends
	Stimulate action
Formulate action	Analyse problems
	Formulate plan for action
	Make decisions
Execute action	Communicate decisions
	Follow up to ensure that action was taken
Amend plan	Replan to ensure all staff work to a current plan
	Replan realistically

Planning structure

It is necessary to adopt a hierarchical planning structure (Figure 26) so that plans and reports are appropriate in detail to the managers who prepare, receive and use them. Typically, the project manager will prepare a series of project control plans, which will be used by him to define and control the work of each of the main contributors.

These plans will be summarised as a project master plan to co-

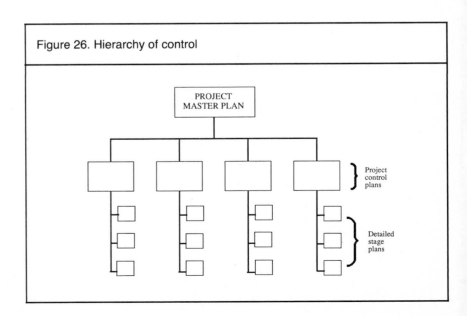

Figure 26. Hierarchy of control

ordinate the work of various contributors, and to report to senior management. At a lower level each contributor will prepare one or more detailed stage/area plans defining how he intends to carry out his work to comply with the targets agreed with the project manager, and shown in the appropriate project control plan.

A staged approach must be taken to the planning, and this requires overall project targets to be established at the project master plan level, with more detailed plans being prepared for each area as they become imminent and adequate information becomes available to substantiate the planning process.

Paths to success

Define requirements

So what is different about IT projects that relate to the single market?

By its very nature IT is deeply interwoven into an organisation. It is the very fabric of the company. When that IT is changed, upgraded or tampered with, the whole organisation is affected. Unlike other services, IT has an intimate relationship with its users. To work properly, IT projects must take serious account of both user requirements and the mechanics of implementation. Defining the requirements to be satisfied by an IT project is one of the most important, yet most difficult, tasks.

Identify the user

A key issue is identifying who the user really is. For example, on a large government project, is the user the recipient of the information, the front-desk clerk, the office manager, the regional manager, the Permanent Secretary, politicians in general, or the Minister? Do one or all of these have to be involved in the definition of the project?

Non-IT aspects are also easily overlooked. Many important IT projects have been threatened because of the shortcomings of the building in which they are to be housed, because the marketing of the service has not been thought through, or most commonly because the impact on people of the new systems has not been properly addressed. Research by the Oxford Institute of Information Management indicates that the most successful IT projects are those developed from existing systems. However, they depend on an overall business strategy being in place first and on the existing IT being sound. 'Don't automate a mess' is the message.

The project management industry is plagued by the problem of an irreducible minimum size, and this type of problem will arise frequently in multi-country 1992 projects. Both advanced technology telecommunications projects and large information systems projects are prone to this. Thus components may be tested individually, but

Risk assessment

the system must reach its final form before it can be tested against the full requirements of the user.

Detailed risk assessment and management, whether included at the cost/benefit analysis stage or in the overall project definition, is critical in managing these situations. The project manager must be aware that risk can arise from many sources that can be broadly classified as:

- Intrinsic risk: i.e. risk arising from factors within the project. This may be subdivided as:
    Managerial (Are all the control processes in place?)
    Execution (Is the plan workable?)
    Technical (Will the system work?)
    Economic (Will the benefits be realised in operation?)

- Extrinsic risk: i.e. risk arising from factors outside the project. This may be subdivided as:
    Business direction (Will the business needs change and/or will the market demands change?)
    Economic (Will the assumptions underlying the cost/benefit case be valid?)
    Technical (Will the new X change the rules?)
    Political (Policy changes)
    Organisational (How does this interact with other projects?)
    Commercial (Will the supplier go bankrupt?)

The specific threats facing a project must be identified and evaluated. Where a specific threat to a project is significant, appropriate counter-measures must be put in place and managed through to completion.

The human dimension – searching for a champion

The complexity of IT projects and the desire to secure user approval at regular intervals demand that a detailed definition of the project is hammered out at the beginning. In this way, it is possible to identify and measure progress and allow management to see light at the end of the tunnel.

But every project needs leadership. This should come from several sources. In addition to the strong voice of approval from the board, IT projects need a totally committed manager who is capable of seeing the business-wide issues, but who at the same time can direct and enthuse the many project leaders, both technical and commercial, who are contributing to the project's success. This manager must be a driver, someone to whom achievement of objectives is all important, and someone who can arouse in his staff the same commitment and determination to succeed. As well as driving forward the work, the champion must ensure that the project team gets the support it needs, and he must defend the team from those people who inevitably denigrate performance and the rationale behind tackling the project.

Champions have been studied in great detail by Cynthia Beath (University of Minnesota) and Blake Ives (Southern Methodist University). As organisations suffer upheaval during an IT programme, the acceptability of that programme can be called into question at many points. From the initial anguished cries of 'It won't work; we don't have the resources; it's just another ego trip; and why don't they leave well enough alone', through to the sullen acceptance of the final result, IT projects are at risk from the company's own staff. Such reactions give some indication of the scale of the problem that current projects experience and which future European-wide programmes will not escape.

Champions operate using information, material resources and management support. Information is used to evaluate, choose and sell an innovation and material resources are necessary to get that information and make a transition. Finally, support is crucial in guaranteeing the resources and securing the rewards for a job well done. Champions accomplish organisational innovation despite having less than the requisite authority or resources. Committed users often make excellent champions. Some champions describe their activities as follows:

- 'It's getting people to have a common view without feeling their turf is being threatened.'

- 'Many IS managers seem to think their role is to play devil's advocate and point out the weaknesses in the proposal.'

- 'It wasn't so much that there was resistance to my idea, but rather that the need was unrecognised – it was a matter of education. Marketing had a problem and engineering had a problem but no one saw that it was possible to solve the problems in one system.'

- 'If we had tried to do this in the normal way of committee meetings, reports and decisions, it would have taken three years instead of six months.'

When the IT director works with the IT champion, rapid progress is usually made. Their advice is:

- 'Sell the idea first. Tell people that you have an idea worth pursuing every time you meet them. Give it relevance, give it momentum. The first thing is to get people interested. The second is to ask whether or not it's feasible.'

- 'Forget cost at the beginning. Try to avoid asking how much and how long. If the costs are reasonable, say you want to do it.'

- 'My philosophy is to keep staff levels stable and just do what can be done with that amount of resource; it cuts down on the less valuable projects or creates pressure to redesign them so they are more valuable.'

Key pre-conditions for success in major European projects

The following are some of the more important factors which must be present if a major multi-country, multi-cutural project is to have a good probability of success:

- Positive parent company and senior management commitment.

- Firm, effective leadership and management from the outset. This means one person in charge with overall authority, having senior active sponsorship available and means the project overcoming departmental or national boundaries.

- Recognition at all times that projects are built by people.

- Clear, comprehensive and properly communicated project definition which covers throroughly all feasibility and design study stages, relates objectives to participants, avoids premature over-commitment, recognises the scale of the task and identifies appropriate organisation for all locations.

- Good planning, clear schedules and adequate back up strategies, covering broad systems aspects, project definition and scope management, a full account of phasing, logistics, environmental and geographical uncertainties and back-up strategies for identified high risk areas.

- Appropriate project organisation which promotes effective team-working through competent people with consistent aims, good horizontal and vertical communications within and outside the project, and sufficient resources.

- Project controls which are simple, visible and 'friendly'.

- Good design and technology management with proper staged tasks prior to final commitment, recognition of the need for interface management, effective change management, recognition of the importance of quality assurance.

- Risk management which recognises the various types of risk but especially external risks – regulation, technology, government, language, culture, etc.

- Full financial analysis of all project risks and availability of funding appraised in relation to perceived success of project at key review points.

- Effective external vendor management covering adequate and relevantly experienced contractors, and contractors made responsible for their performance without unfair penalties for events outside their control.

Summary

Bringing the IT project in on time may prove more difficult in Europe than on familiar UK ground. A recent survey in the UK indicated that 46 per cent of a nationwide sample of IT projects were completed late and 48 per cent of them exceeded their budgets. A strong correlation was established between high costs and short timescales. Technical incompetence, the survey found, was rarely found to have affected the project's fate.

The scope for cost overruns and project delays will increase as we move closer to 1992 and in line with the number of European markets in which the organisation is attempting to establish a presence or market a product. Those companies that have experience of overseas project work will be well placed to expand this into full-blown Continent-wide programmes, while others may be more at ease adopting a piece-meal approach with pilot projects in one country or market which eventually lead to a pan-European strategy.

In order to address these problems, considerable emphasis must be given to the management environment of the projects. The approach must:

- Develop a project culture

- Impose discipline
- Achieve visibility through effective controls
- Bring the right people to the right tasks

This is achieved by focusing on the project management plan supported by the most appropriate control systems, sound risk management and dedicated project champions. With this approach it is possible to ensure that the basis of project management is always in sight. Always remember, projects exist to deliver benefits.

11.   The way ahead

There can be little doubt that UK industry faces one of the greatest challenges since the end of the Second World War. Although many view and respond to the challenge differently, it is widely agreed that the relatively cosy world we live in will cease to exist by 1992 at the latest, and probably a lot sooner.

There are two simple facts facing industry: first, the single market lies ahead of us and will not go away. A radical overhaul of organisational attitudes and infrastructure will be necessary for the UK to compete successfully against her European partners during the next decade. Second, IT holds the key to effecting this overhaul and preparing the company for the next generation of trading conditions as created by the single market.

If a company or a chief executive understands the magnitude of the 1992 challenge and accepts the phenomenal range of solutions that IT offers, the most important step in moving the organisation into the mainstream of the next century's business life has been taken. Hand-in-hand with this acceptance of 1992 and IT goes the recognition that the immediate future involves much hard work in restructuring the organisation, considerable investment in new technologies, a vast expenditure of energy and analysis, perhaps an occasional minor failure, but ultimately success in delivering new products and services to demanding customers not only in the EC but globally.

The global scene

Many industries already operate in global markets where economies of scale are crucial to compensate for the enormous R&D costs of their products. Aerospace was one of the first modern industrial sectors that was forced to look to an international market to justify the expenditure of new aircraft R&D. This was followed by the car industry and then by defence electronics.

The UK's shipbuilding industry operated on an international level simply because the size of the Royal Navy and its geographical dispersion permitted large economies of scale. UK shipbuilders began to look abroad for a large portion of their order books and started to create more universal products only when the size of the Royal Navy began to shrink. As markets have become more international in their outlook, companies have had to reflect this in their structure.

Despite their rivalry, the Japanese, US and European IT industries are mutually dependent while Europe's IT companies rely on the US and Japan for the supply of many basic electronic components and systems. The total European IT market (hardware and software) exceeds $100 billion a year and is expected to grow by at least 10 to 15 per cent annually during the next decade.

While the chief executive of one of Europe's leading office IT companies may say that Europe is not the ideal place for the development of cutting-edge IT, few countries exist where 'ideal' conditions persist for any length of time. That Europe still has an IT industry at all, we should be grateful.

European solutions

Work by the EC and by ESPRIT has helped partially to stem the tide of Japanese and US influence in IT procurement. Europe has the chance to find European solutions to its IT problems and it has the opportunity of bringing about the radical transformation of its collective economies through European technology. ESPRIT's success has been in encouraging cross-border co-operation to create much needed pan-European standards and to develop new technologies. In all of these areas, ESPRIT has managed to make important advances and has instilled a new sense of community among IT companies and individuals.

Developments in IT

In spite of the growth of IT as a critical factor in modern business life, there have been a number of important barriers to the wider use of IT. These have included:

- Incompatible, multi-vendor environments

- Hierarchical and proprietary networks

- The high cost of ownership

- An inability to move data between applications and databases

- A confusing variety of 'unfriendly' user interfaces

Standardisation

Fortunately, there has been a realisation by IT vendors that they must standardise their products, but the enormity of this task has taken its toll and many suppliers still pay lip-service to the concept rather than take decisive action. One of the emerging standards is UNIX, which started life in the early 1970s in the Bell Laboratories of AT&T and has since turned into a battleground for a clash of computer Titans that will streamline the choice of options available on the market today.

The continuing debate over proprietary systems and open systems may affect the strategy of an organisation. Many organisations are now faced with making choices about what type of IT they will use for the next decade. Unfortunately, the outcome of the UNIX debate is not linked to the Commission's 1992 timetable.

Incompatible technologies are a luxury that few companies can afford in the single market. Companies cannot afford to run the risk of creating artificial barriers within the organisation or of tying one hand behind their back in the fight with competitors. The transition between proprietary and open systems may be difficult, but the advantages will repay the effort.

Open systems offer the degree of flexibility that will be a pre-requisite for conducting business efficiently into the next century. In an open computing environment, companies will be able to plan coherent strategies that reflect commercial realities rather than experience knee-jerk reactions to the latest whim of software or hardware suppliers. The only significant drawback in open systems at the moment is the lack of large-scale experience. Managements may feel they are being asked to jump on yet another bandwagon that fails to head for the sunset at the end of the trail. The most effective way to cope with such uncertainty is to monitor the progress of open systems and match that progress with the right resources. If progress is slow, investment planning should remain modest. However, if progress is rapid, a company must be able to keep pace with developments or it may lose its competitive advantage.

Aligning strategy

The foundation of any company's activities is its strategy. The strategy formulation process becomes more complicated when introducing a viable IT strategy coincides with preparations for 1992. The root of strategic planning will be understanding the 'competitive position' of the organisation. A combined 1992/IT strategy will need to examine:

- Proposed regulatory changes in the EC

- Current and future EC customer requirements

- Competitor activity

- Supplier activity

- Market size and segmentation

The focus of the organisation's activities will be the customer and successful strategy implementation will depend on harnessing the collective energy of the company.

Offensive/defensive strategies

Strategies for 1992 can be broadly divided into offensive and defensive strategies. The offensive organisation oozes with entrepreneurial zeal and is viewed warily by its competitors. It has an overview of the 1992 market and is prepared to revamp its entire organisation from top to bottom to accommodate the single European market. The defensive company, on the other hand, sees 1992 as a threat. Frequently stuck in traditionally weak industries that have faced little competition or change in demand for years, these companies possess long-term strategies that are often out-of-date or unclear. They lack any vision of a united Europe. Realising which category your company belongs to is an early step towards recognising how much work must be done before an effective IT-based 1992 strategy can be defined and implemented.

The IT strategy can be viewed as:

- Warding off competitive threats

- Meeting corporate objectives

- Measuring and improving performance

- Keeping senior management informed

IT will help change the face of Europe in the next decade, and the converse must also be encouraged. Greater demands have to be placed on IT professionals and vendors to produce systems that have the flexibility to cope with the changes that everyone knows lie ahead.

A recent survey concluded that the typical UK company makes 'significant use of information technology for operational and administrative support and suffers from fragmented systems and data. It has a medium-term strategy for development of new computer systems, which is driven for business objective and the search for competitive and strategic advantage . . . its strategy is usually aimed at cost reductions and productivity improvement.' This is not necessarily a recipe for success in 1992.

If there is any simple starting point for a business strategy, it is quality. Corporate and IT strategies are subsets of the much broader strategy of quality, which identifies the customer as the single most important factor in the operations of the entire organisation – everything is geared towards achieving customer satisfaction and anything that inhibits this must be eliminated.

Build in quality

Europe has been almost a decade late in recognising the importance of building quality into the organisation and the products that it makes from the very start. Quality begins long before raw materials are ordered or staff are hired to place that order. It starts as a management frame of mind which diffuses into every single operation of the organisation – from answering telephones to parking customers' cars, from reviewing existing work methods to planning future product lines that match customer needs more closely, from producing a workforce that is proud to say it works for your company to producing customers who know they are buying quality products and services that have first-rate after-sales care, should they need it.

Products

The daily test of an organisation's ability to succeed in Europe after 1992 will be the acceptability of its products or services not only in its own historic market but in the domestic markets of the Continent. Customer buying patterns are already changing – increasing pressure on the life-cycle of products and the growing difficulty in establishing new brands in a packed market place have placed new pressures on companies to innovate. If a company fails to keep pace with the innovation rate of its competitors, it will find itself seriously disadvantaged. Simultaneous innovation for six or eight major markets or sub-markets in Europe requires a dramatic overhaul in the way organisations view their R&D programmes. It is no longer a matter of talking about a new product for two years, taking a further two years to develop it and expecting it to have a market life of fifteen to twenty years or so. Experience with new product innovations indicates there is a tightening of the basic rules. There is less time to innovate because markets are changing all the time, less opportunity to produce the products before the competition copies them, and a greater chance of product failure because of the growing complexity of customer demands and perceptions.

Innovation by simulation

IT offers a company the chance to innovate by simulation and to integrate the R&D function so that there is less wasted research effort. Computer-aided design has already established itself as a vital component in the car industry for new model development and has

Sourcing opportunities

trimmed vital months off crucial design stages so that new marques are available six months to a year earlier than when more conventional methods were used.

R&D that is inspired by IT and geared towards 1992 will be able to examine the possible combinations of new materials from different European suppliers as the sourcing of components becomes more diverse. Similarly it will be able to produce working examples of the product or system earlier than has previously been possible. Production engineering centered on an IT platform will enable a company to select the right location in Europe for the actual manufacture of the new product and will permit a greater variety of sub-assemblies. This will be necessary when products are being geared towards different markets. A greater emphasis on simplicity of design will occur as engineering teams try to increase automation in their manufacturing processes. At the same time, the marketing department will place pressure on the design department to enhance the features of the product range so that further market share can be won.

An imaginative approach to IT is the one important means of reconciling these very different influences.

Quality manufacturing

Not only must we start thinking about new products for the single market, but also we must start looking at building the factory that will produce them. UK management must be appalled at the public relations image that manufacturing still has in the UK today. Starved of bright, innovative graduates, manufacturing has had to soldier on in the hope that help would arrive before the more glamorous professions cut off its supply of new blood completely.

In manufacturing today there have been countless advances achieved through the use of IT. Whereas the general public may see an alphabet soup of manufacturing disciplines, senior management sees rapid development of production techniques offering greater rewards for those prepared to think and innovate their way out of difficulty and into profitability. Computer-aided design and computer-aided manufacturing (CAD/CAM) have been redefined and moulded into something even more exciting – computer-integrated manufacturing (CIM). Here a particular formula of IT has been specifically prepared for an organisation to allow it to take an overview of its entire design, sourcing, production, distribution and marketing operations. Everything is interlocked and dovetailed into everything else. The company achieves the flexibility and responsiveness to changing market conditions that will be the hallmark of successful organisations after 1992.

Quest for the office of tomorrow

Despite the apparent high levels of investment in IT that have taken place in offices over the past twenty years, the modern office is still in a backwater. Research labs bristle with new inventions, and production lines have fully automated armies of robots. The office still has the humble, and frequently humbled, white-collar worker waiting for the revolution that seems to have passed by his window. Two hundred years of office routine have taken their toll. But the office, as we know it, will probably cease to exist in the next twenty years.

The upheaval that 1992 will create is only the beginning of a whole series of major readjustments that organisations can expect to make during the lifetime of most senior executives. Within years, our office infrastructure will be expected to handle huge volumes of data, interpret and develop these into a form of knowledge and communicate them to benefit the organisation. Such an architecture will require a flawless IT system that can cope with changes in the quality and availability of information while remaining relevant to users, expandable for future development and supportable by its IT staff. The 1992 office will need to handle multi-currency invoicing, produce sales literature in at least three languages other than English, support products in a variety of countries, react rapidly to changing local circumstances and provide senior management with a pan-European measure of performance. In order to achieve this near-Herculean task, management will rely increasingly on the quality of their staff to effect these changes.

The human dimension

So much has been written about the quality of technology in the past that the people who operate it are often forgotten, taken for granted or lumped into the 'end-user' or 'firm-ware' category that exists somewhere between hardware and software. The activities of every member of the organisation have an extra dimension and an extra impact as both the domestic market and the European scene change in the run up to 1992. IT allows management to achieve goals and employees to make a worthwhile contribution to the company for which they work.

Strategies must be flexible

Every organisation has some form of business strategy. This strategy will be the guiding light for everyone in the company, but it is no longer adequate to gather together in a country mansion once every five years and formulate a corporate plan of action. Strategies must be treated like living organisms that change shape as circumstances change. They must be watched, nurtured, modified, or, if necessary, scrapped if the situation demands it. This demands active management of the strategy by senior executives. The board must lead the organisation through periods of change and risk, some of which may be self-inflicted. Management's ability to cope with change will be put to the test long before the rest of the workforce's, and if the top levels of the organisation cannot handle this change the rank and file cannot be expected to.

Human resource management

It has taken UK management a long time to accept that the human resource element of the organisation can offer competitive advantage and that the modification of internal structures and training can be used to improve the company's human resource development. As markets and organisations become more global in their outlook, there will be increased pressure on personnel to adopt a more international approach. An increased emphasis will be placed on multi-lingual abilities, geographically and culturally diverse educational backgrounds and an internationally oriented career path. Staff will be expected to move more frequently around the organisation, both departmentally and geographically. Increased emphasis may need to be placed on graduate recruitment, particularly from abroad, while training of new recruits will need to be more carefully structured.

The international approach

Women

Changing work patterns will make it desirable to rehire staff that have left to rear families. A large-scale rehiring of 28- to 45-year-old women is one of the few ways open to UK industry of dealing with the demographic time-bomb ticking away in our society. French and German labour law is heavily geared to encouraging young mothers back to work. Our attitudes towards women, although not quite as medieval as Japan's, need swift and radical change before acute skilled-labour shortages develop in the mid-1990s. There may even be a case for aggressive recruitment of young Japanese female technicians and white-collar workers, since they are virtually excluded from the levels of management that women have attained in Europe and the USA. If there was ever one single competitive advantage that can be gained easily over Japanese industrial rivals, it is non-discriminatory employment practices.

Respect employee aspirations

As labour becomes more mobile, companies will need to accommodate a broader range of employee aspirations. Some European cultures are less individualist than others and employees expect more direction from superiors than UK workers might. Similarly, some European nationalities do not place the same importance on pay as UK workers but are more concerned about the quality of the work environment and a caring approach from the management. A mixture of nationalities and differing outlooks on pay and conditions will enrich any organisation and infuse into its culture the much needed European dimension.

The challenge facing us in Europe is largely one of temperament, culture, language difference, customs and perhaps even ethics. The common denominator to all of these is people. A company that has a sizeable proportion of its staff recruited from outside the UK, that has a collective body of knowledge that spans numerous – preferably European – cultures, that has fostered cross-departmental and geographic mobility, that rewards individual and collective efforts, that encourages innovation and does not punish failure, and that engenders a positive culture where people and their ideas can thrive: this is a company that will succeed in the single market. Organisations that lack any or all of these attributes must dismantle outdated perceptions and start from the beginning.

Through numerous small and large IT projects, there will gradually evolve a truly European organisation.

IT will be in the vanguard of the battle to achieve and hold competitive advantage because it offers the chance to straddle cultural and linguistic boundaries. The case for open multi-vendor systems will become more apparent as time passes and the critical need for flexibility of approach and response increases.

The first basic steps to using IT as a means of meeting the European single market challenge are:

- Get a decision to implement an effective IT strategy from the top of the organisation.

- Evaluate how your products and the running of your business can be improved through IT. If this proves difficult, imagine what your competition would do with the same opportunity.

- Develop an IT strategy that is linked to your overall business strategy. If no one is responsible for IT in your company, appoint someone and give him/her board-level status.

- Decide what you want from IT and give the goals of greater productivity, cost reduction or improved levels of service an order of priority.

- Check your goals are being achieved. Three-month, six-month and annual reviews of new and old IT systems should be considered.

- Become computer literate.

- Be patient. It may take two years before real progress is discernible.

- Challenge all basic assumptions, even the need for an IT investment, during the formulation of the original strategy and the subsequent reviews.

IT can be all things to all men. Publisher Robert Maxwell views it as 'a way not only to automate business transactions but also to improve the timeliness and quality of management decisions'. Others are trying to achieve the goal of a paperless office. John Harvey-Jones, when chairman of ICI, viewed IT as a means of changing ICI's corporate culture. A leading executive of a major US oil company points out: 'We do not know what the technology will be like in the future but we know it will be very different, that the opportunities it creates will be significant and that senior management will have to make changes to meet these challenges.'

IV
Case studies

Introduction

Building effective IT applications is a slow process. Developing the applications necessary for the single market is a process few organisations have yet begun to tackle in detail. Our case studies are therefore not drawn from the leading edge. Instead we have chosen to show how recent, well-managed IT developments prepare a company to perform more effectively in a competitive environment. We have selected a broad range of case studies to show how the discussions in earlier chapters can be translated into positive action. Having implemented a range of changes, these companies will be better placed to respond to the single market challenge.

The case studies illustrate that IT can be approached in numerous ways and that the benefits of a carefully developed IT strategy will also vary considerably. Consolidating an existing market position, improving internal efficiency or striking deep at the heart of the competition: all are possible with IT. It is, however, crucial to see IT as a specific enabling process rather than a one-shot cure-all. It is a process that should not be set in motion lightly. IT has an important role to play in revitalising the health of UK and European industry. As 1992 approaches, the IT casebook will hopefully bulge with more examples of inspired applications of IT, which will have transformed the nation's corporate health.

Shell Chemicals finds the right formula

Shell Chemicals UK (SCUK) used the move to a new head office as a catalyst for upgrading their IT. Planning and implementation took place over a two-year period, during which time SCUK moved its head office from London to Chester. The new head office was planned with a very low number of support staff, and it was envisaged that integrated office systems would play a significant part in the running of the office. The office systems project included painting the picture of the future (the strategy) and bringing it to fruition (the implementation). Later, the effectiveness of the changes brought about by an integrated information system used by everyone at SCUK head office was independently reviewed.

Business background

SCUK is one of three companies operating in the UK belonging to the Royal Dutch Shell Group. It has major manufacturing sites in Cheshire and Greater Manchester, a head office in Chester, and sales staff in other major cities. In mid-1986, SCUK commissioned a fundamental review of the organisation. The aim of this review was to indicate ways in which the organisation could best prepare itself for the next decade, particularly to maintain the improvements in business perfomance then being reported.

The major changes which were identified by this review as potential contributors to the future health of the business were:

- Increased informality of communication
- Improved access to communication systems
- A corporate rather than divisional identity

All in all, a very significant culture change.

Office automation at SCUK

To support the changes necessary to provide these improvements, SCUK considered the introduction of a company-wide office automation system. The project involved:

- Defining the strategy and selecting the most suitable system
- Designing and managing an extensive education and training programme
- Implementing the system
- Identifying corporate and departmental applications
- Developing applications to supplement the base functions
- Integrating the office automation facilities with the extensive range of data systems which already existed

An office systems team was set up. This team's purpose was to maximise the impact of office systems on the whole SCUK organisation. This involved selecting the system and the strategy for its implementation, ensuring that the chosen system performed well and in a way which best served the business and those who worked in it. The team's work continued after the completion of the initial installation and training exercise. A framework for regular monitoring of the system was provided to determine its performance and the benefits achieved. In summer 1988, a formal review of these benefits was carried out.

The strategy was developed by a small team. Many interviews were carried out, along with an analysis of communication flows using conventional means. These led to a strategy that ensured SCUK's integration with the rest of the Shell Group, but allowed it to add the applications which it had identified as essential to the overall success of the systems. The strategy also included provision for very close intercommunications with the company's extensive management information systems.

The team's greatest contribution was to ensure that the implementation was successful. The climate was right, with an enthusiastic chief executive, and a brand new office building on the way, and this good climate was exploited with well-directed work on two fronts. The users attended seminars which presented the vision and the importance of office automation to SCUK's future; they were given detailed training and personal follow-up visits. Technically, the work was directed towards providing the central mainframe service and adding extra applications. Close liaison with users, the effectiveness of the training and the reliable delivery of new systems allowed the development team to hand over an effective working system, well-satisfied users, and an extensive shopping list of new requirements and enhancements.

Another aspect was evaluation. Despite managing important aspects of a tight implementation schedule, the team ensured that it was able to stand back and identify action needed to improve the implementation process – continuous constructive evaluation. Benefits do not materialise just with the introduction of the system. There has to be a programme of realisation, managed, like any other complex programme, with direction from the top.

Technical success is only a part of the story. The board, their senior managers, and their staff are convinced that not only has the office system changed the way they work (for the better) but it has helped the business. And it provides a platform for the future – an efficient organisation can compete at any level. A culture attuned to immediate response across electronic mail networks considers Bonn to be as near as Birmingham, Lisbon as near as Liverpool. Shell's network already covers their prime sites on the Continent.

The system paid for itself in just over a year, and that despite heavy investment in the people and organisational aspects of the changes – aspects often forgotten in the drive for a technical solution. The approach taken by SCUK, and the benefits to individuals and the business, show the power of office computing and the foundation it can give for future business success.

In their own words

'The introduction of the integrated information system has been a great success; the system has helped all staff in corporate functions respond to the challenges presented by the upturn in the chemicals business. All staff are now able to work more closely with customers; there is an improved information flow and quality within sales and business teams and also between sites.'

'With the rapid growth in the world chemicals business in recent years, future success will be determined by each company's ability to meet the challenges of the next decade and with the help of the information network, Shell Chemicals is now in a much stronger position to respond rapidly to that upturn in the market.'

The electronic revolution which has been quietly taking place throughout Shell Chemicals during the last twelve months has reaped enormous benefits for staff and customers alike. Shell Chemicals' office automation system is a standard-setter for the rest of UK industry.

Lawrence Graham judges the case for IT

Since the middle of 1986, Lawrence Graham has been developing its use of computing gradually but effectively. Driven by a level of informed management commitment not found in many other organisations, the law practice moved from mixed, incompatible typewriters and accounting systems to a single, firm-wide integrated system. Now, partners, solicitors and secretaries can work together on legal matters, on billing and time recording, and on the management of the firm. Partners themselves use the system and are convinced that the investment has been worthwhile.

Lawrence Graham is a medium-sized (thirty-five partners) firm of London solicitors, with a typical mix of work – commercial, litigation, conveyancing, tax, trust and probate, and particular specialism in Eastern bloc shipping. The story begins, aptly enough, with the Department of Trade and Industry's 'Britain has IT' roadshow in early 1986. At that time, Lawrence Graham had several offices around Lincoln's Inn, but was considering a move to a single office to improve internal communications and to present the desired image to their potential clients – a move completed in 1986. The firm had grasped the need to market itself more consistently, to make more effective use of what it already had – staff, information and expertise. 'Britain has IT' arrived at the right time to spark the development of the information component.

Two things characterised Lawrence Graham's move into IT – management commitment and, in parallel, the realisation that effective use of IT was a management, not a technical, issue. These two threads have continued through the three years of practice development. From the initial question of 'Tell me what IT can do for me?', through supplier selection, implementation and diffusion of the system, there has been belief at senior partner level that such systems were essential to the long-term health of the firm.

The investment has brought benefits:

- Electronic mail has helped the partnership become more unified

- Direct access to accounting data has improved billing and cash flow

- Existing client information has been used to generate new business for different departments within the firm

- Trust, tax and litigation departments can use shared personal computer systems to provide a better service to clients

- Partners have more control over their (expensive) time because the administration of the firm has been simplified

- Responsiveness to clients has increased through ready access to precedents and the extra flexibility in the secretarial service

- The firm presents a consistent, and modern, image to its clients

- Several staff have developed to fulfil their potential and contribute more fully to the firm

- Good legal staff are attracted to a firm which can demonstrate the most up-to-date support services

Computers do not make Lawrence Graham better lawyers, but they help them to be more effective. As a business, it helps the firm provide the necessary service at the necessary profit levels. As with all management processes, there is no end. Lawrence Graham is already addressing two key issues likely to affect the legal world in the next decade: competition and staff. The Lord Chancellor hopes to open up the legal world – Lawrence Graham's effective and efficient support base gives it the platform from which to compete.

As is well known, the number of new entrants to the job market is falling. This is as true of trained solicitors as it is of engineers, accountants or administrators. Lawrence Graham intends to use technology to provide the best possible working environment in the office. Beyond that, the firm can increase the potential work pool by providing access to people working from home.

This firm was faced with an upheaval at least as great as that which will be caused by the pan-European market of 1992. Its investment in, and commitment to, IT has placed it in a strong position to compete in new markets and to recruit and retain the staff which, in the professions, are essential if that competition is to be effective. Whatever additional opportunities and competition the single market brings, Lawrence Graham is well placed to respond.

Mail Newspapers: read all about IT

In 1996 the *Daily Mail*, Britain's first popular national newspaper, will celebrate its centenary. From its launch, the *Daily Mail* and, very much later, the *Mail on Sunday*, have been printed at a site near Fleet Street. During that time equipment, production methods and culture changed very little, with union branches maintaining formidable control over employment and production. In 1985, Project 2000 was launched by Mail Newspapers. This was to be a breakout strategy, involving the complete relocation of the editorial and advertising functions to Kensington, in West London, and the production facilities to a greenfield site in London's Docklands. The main goals of Project 2000 were to:

- Reduce costs dramatically through the use of the new highly automated production plant, new editorial and advertising systems and a responsive and flexible organisation

- Improve the quality of the product through the introduction of colour flexographic printing presses

- Reduce the time from completion of editorial to start of print

- Maintain Mail Newspapers' leading position in an extremely competitive and dynamic industry

- Implement computer-based systems which would provide accurate and timely information, enabling management to control the business more effectively

Harmsworth Quays Printing Limited, as the new production site is called, is responsible for the day-to-day operation of arguably one of the world's most technically advanced newspaper printing and distribution plants. From the arrival of the paper reels to the despatch of printed newpapers, computers monitor and control every process. A high degree of automation and computer integration is necessary to minimise manpower costs and improve reliability and integrity of data transfer.

Reel delivery and storage

A fleet of specially designed articulated container trucks delivers reels of paper, each fifty inches in diameter and weighing up to 1.8 tonnes, to the plant. A full load of eighteen reels can be off-loaded in forty-five seconds. As the reels enter the multi-storey paper store, each is automatically sized, weighed and checked for damage. Data from each reel is read from a barcode by laser scanners that provide vital information on size, grade, supplier and paper mill. As reels are tracked throughout the plant, quality, yield and performance problems can be traced back to supplier and batch number.

The reel store is fully automated and can hold up to 1,000 reels, with a computer control system to show instantly where each reel is located and its precise details. Three automatic cranes operating in the warehouse can move up to 170 reels in and out of the store every working hour.

Reel preparation

The press management computer in the heart of the complex receives the total pagination for individual editions and the number of presses that will be printing them. In turn, the automatic guided vehicle (AGV) computer instructs the reel store to deliver the precise number and size of reels to the preparation area where reels are stripped of their outer wrapper and again checked for damage. The reels for production go directly from the preparation station to the press hall via a fleet of eighteen AGVs. Guided by wires set underfloor, the AGVs deliver precisely on time before reels are expended. This allows all eight presses to run uninterrupted.

The press hall

There are eight Koenig and Bauer flexographic presses in two parallel lines of four, providing a total capacity of over half a million newspapers per hour. Each press has up to five reel stands with each stand taking three reels of paper. As one reel runs out, the 'spider' holding the reels rotates and the next new reel is automatically joined to the old one, without interrupting production.

A major decision was made, early in the project, to implement flexographic technology. Amid the virtual monopoly of web-offset newspaper printing in the UK this was a bold move. It offered, however, a number of compelling competitive advantages: faster start-ups, hence reduced lead time from editorial to print; improved and more consistent print quality through the use of water based inks with no rub-off and less show through; excellent colour quality; reduced running and material costs.

Plate making

All pre-press material originates at New Northcliffe House in Kensington, where the editorial and advertising functions operate. A computer-controlled facsimile transmission system delivers whole, ready-for-press pages over a data network to Harmsworth Quays. The fax negatives (or laser masks) arriving at Harmsworth Quays are manually fed into platemaking machines, which produce a photo polymer resin printing-plate. A computer system ensures that the plates leaving each platemaking machine are identified and marked with a barcode so that a computer-controlled plate conveyor can pick them up automatically and deliver them instantly to the correct press.

Publishing and distribution

Before each production run, the circulation department collates all the sales orders and enters them into its computer system. A consolidated requirements list is then transferred automatically to the publishing computer system. Using this system, delivery runs, vehicles and despatch times can be planned in advance and then amended to take account of actual changes in volumes and production factors.

Conveyors deliver printed newspapers from the presses into the publishing hall where they are counted, stacked, labelled, wrapped and finally, strapped. A barcode printed on the label allows the bundles to be routed, using interlinking conveyors, to a defined outlet and into a waiting van.

Newspaper production demands exceptional reliability – unless copies can be produced on time, meeting strict delivery schedules to get the final product to newsagents, sales will be lost. The company identified several vital requirements during the early stages of the project, which were to become the basis of a CIM strategy and the development of specifications. These requirements were:

- All key items of computer hardware were to be replicated and configured in a 'warm' standby operation

- Where data communications between devices were essential, any networking would be replicated or alternate paths configured

- All critical single points of failure would be eliminated as far as practical

- Production must not stop as a result of any computer failure

It is not feasible to implement a major CIM project of this kind in one step. The technical, cultural and educational demands dictate a gradual step-by-step approach. An implementation plan was developed based on the following stages:

- Installation and commissioning of all separate process computer systems to enable full stand-alone operation

- Installation of the network and all interfacing devices

- Commissioning of peer-to-peer communication

- Development, installation and commissioning of the MIS

- Integration of stand-alone systems with the MIS, to transfer real-time production information and end-of-shift reports for management attention

In parallel with all the technical development, Mail Newspapers undertook a major computer awareness programme to prepare every employee for the introduction of new technology and the associated cultural change. It developed a top down programme from a five-day residential course of senior management to more intensive one or two-day courses for operators and engineers. Almost every person to be involved at Harmsworth Quays attended one of the courses to gain experience of using computers and develop an understanding of the new technology and its implications.

The first of the eight new presses went into operation, on schedule, in the autumn of 1988. When fully commissioned, the plant will be highly responsive and flexible in order to meet the increasing demands of the reader and the advertiser at the lowest possible cost. The enormous technological and cultural changes the company has gone through during this project are now beginning to deliver major benefit to the business. Whether foreign language editions ever run off the press is an interesting speculation but, in terms of showing how to use technology as a catalyst for change, Mail Newspapers has shown the way for a range of companies inside and outside the print industry.

Car makers gear up for change

European car manufacturing has proven to be a valuable test-bed for the advanced uses of IT. The experience of at least two major car makers provides a guide to some of the areas in which IT can be applied but also yields an insight into the strategic thinking that may be needed by manufacturers after 1992. Volvo and Ford Europe are cited in *Information Management – the Strategic Dimension* (Michael Earl, Clarendon Press, 1988) as working examples of what IT can do, given the right environment. Yet each company approached IT from different angles and naturally derived different benefits.

Volvo

Established in 1927, Volvo has evolved into one of Sweden's leading industrial groups with activities ranging from the manufacture of cars and trucks to aerospace, food, energy and trading interests. Two-thirds of group turnover, however, comes from the dominant automotive side. The group is a Swedish-based international operation with 74 per cent of the workforce in Sweden and 82 per cent of revenue (excluding oil) coming from abroad.

At the heart of Volvo's commitment to IT is Volvo Data AB, formed after a major reorganisation of the company in 1972. The subsidiary was set up to operate as an allocated cost centre providing systems development services and data-processing operations to the entire group. It was expected to compete with outside computer service groups but also to offer superior pricing. The company, which employs 600 people, provides about 40 per cent of the total IT services to the group today.

Volvo Data's processing power is about 140 mips and storage capacity is almost one terrabyte (1 million million bytes). Over 17,000 terminals are plugged into its network. The group has a decentralised structure with each unit responsible for its own results. Directives and guidelines such as common standards for IT still emanate from headquarters. Common IT standards were established because of the need for a holistic view on the use of IT and because it is a relatively expensive, rapidly changing, resource. Underpinning all of this was the need for integration of information throughout the entire company.

Vertical business integration and the need for detailed information at different levels of the organisation have been, according to Karl-Henrik Hubinette of Volvo Data, the driving force for the development of common systems. The whole concept of distributed common systems was made possible by an early standardisation of computer equipment for the group's network of overseas agents. A dozen different systems have been installed in Volvo's major foreign importers and dealer systems have been installed in over 100 dealerships.

Two major advantages have been gained from this common systems approach. There has been a major improvement in the data about available spare parts and accessories at both the dealer and importer level giving the main parts department in Sweden a chance to optimise its production planning. Since the capital tied up in the central storage of parts by importers and dealers represents a large portion of the cost of the parts distribution chain, any reduction in stock levels would be a major advantage. IT has improved the profitability of the parts division, by optimising warehousing and distribution, and has kept prices competitive for customers.

The same common system approach has been used in the handling of warranty claims on new cars. Verification and acceptance of warranty claims must be processed in a uniform manner worldwide. Volvo dealers and car owners know instantly if a claim under the warranty has been accepted, while the manufacturing plants will be aware of product quality problems and be able to correct faults on the production line, thereby cutting future claims.

'The continuing proliferation of data-processing in our organisation further compounds the problem of management and control of IT,' Hubinette explains. 'We have more than 100 mini and maxi computers in our various companies. There is a growing understanding in the boardrooms and in the executive suites that IT may have a great impact on the business itself and that the conventional data-processing organisation and its manager cannot be expected to handle the strategic planning of IT on their own. We feel that there is a growing acceptance on the part of company management that a well thought out and formulated strategy for IT is necessary. Also there is a realisation that information can be an important company resource and that the proper use of this resource is dependent on accepted standards being followed throughout the organisation.

'Management should take full responsibility for the role that IT will have in the organisation and determine the criteria for performance and effectiveness. The data-processing organisation can then concentrate on being a professional support centre, responsible for maintaining high efficiency in computer and communications processing and having the technological expertise required by the business. There are no signs that the present development in IT will stop or even slow down in the foreseeable future.'

Ford

Ford Europe uses its IT in a different way. The company sees its main challenge as carving out a viable, profitable business into the next decade, despite forecasts of a relatively static European market. Nissan, with its plant at Washington, England, is viewed as a particular threat to Ford's goals. Confronted with substantial overcapacity in Europe, Ford developed strategies to cut costs and bring products to the market more rapidly.

According to Graham Gooding of Ford in Europe, the company concentrated on five areas: improving quality, raising margins, reducing fixed cost, investing in human resource management and pursuing joint ventures.

Computer-aided design (CAD) and computer-aided manufacturing (CAM) were the main planks in Ford's platform for success. There was a population explosion of robots on the factory floor. The head count, which numbered 106 in 1980, soared to 1,350 in five years and is still growing significantly each year. Encouraged by gains that Japanese industry had made in time, quality and productivity, Ford accelerated its CAD/CAM investment as a response to the Japanese competitive threat. This led the company to consider developing strategic plans and moving into a more sophisticated business environment – computer-integrated manufacturing, where all the processes in a highly automated factory are integrated and the same data is shared by planners, schedulers, foremen, designers and engineers (see Chapter 6).

Product development, says Gooding, started with twenty-eight CAD workstations in 1981 and is expected to have 300 by the end of the decade. With each new model, the CAD component is increased. The Sierra, launched in 1982, had 8 per cent of the design aided by computers while the Scorpio had a 25 per cent CAD component. By 1992, Ford hopes to be able to sell cars that have had up to 90 per cent of their design work done by computers.

Programme lead time in product development, a critical element in the car industry, has been cut by two months for the body tooling of a new model. Prototype model manufacture has seen even greater gains. Ford's compatible CAD/CAM strategies worldwide allow joint design exercises with operations in the USA and Australia and is now being extended to some suppliers. Huge volumes of CAD data are transmitted between the UK and West Germany. These traffic flows are expected to rise rapidly, particularly when the link with suppliers is strengthened.

In manufacturing, Ford started with one CAM workstation in 1981 and is expected to have over 280 in place by 1992. Computer automation in sheet-metal die design, die model manufacturing and die manufacturing has slashed four months off the design cycle.

CIM has offered Ford the prospect of integrating vehicle manufacture across Europe, planning production at individual plants, monitoring actual on-site output, quality and maintenance and control of computer-controlled units such as factory robots. 'Increasingly effective telecommunications', says Gooding, 'will be of critical importance here.' The link with suppliers will be strengthened by the weekly electronic transmission of six-month production schedules, daily advice of ten-day production line-ups and Just-In-Time deliveries.

Ford has also been trying to get closer to its customers with its European-wide parts distribution system. The company claims to be the only car maker in Europe that recommends a particular computing system to its dealers, which provides point of sale, inventory management and management services. It hopes to have 1,000 dealers in ten countries – representing about half of all the vehicle and parts business – on the system soon.

'We are no longer constrained by technology,' asserts Gooding. 'There is merit in being at the leading edge. It is a time for boldness, a time for encouraging innovation, a time for rewarding creativity. But we are constrained by our company culture, organisation and people issues. Our ability to respond to technological changes is moving at a much slower rate than the technology itself. Tomorrow's winners will have encouraged innovation and creativity in exploiting technology, but to be winners they will also have found new and inventive ways to deliver these technologies.'

Sainsbury's: checking out the potential

Sainsbury's, the largest UK supermarket operator, embarked on an ambitious programme of IT development in the early 1980s, designed to support rapid growth of the business. Coupled with this was a clear-cut determination to secure a competitive advantage over its rivals in the highly competitive UK grocery retailing sector.

Over 7 million customers shop at Sainsbury's each week, giving it almost 11 per cent of national food and drink sales, and it is the UK's largest retailer in a number of areas, including wine, fresh produce and meat. It is one of the most successful retailers in the world, with profits growth of 20 per cent or more in each of the last ten years. Sainsbury's was the first of the UK supermarket groups to make the move to central distribution, setting up a network of owned and contracted distribution warehouses some years ago, to which suppliers deliver. A fleet of over 750 trucks then delivers to the stores, with most stores receiving several deliveries every day. As well as reducing costs, this has greatly improved the availability of stock on the store shelf and contributed in a major way to Sainsbury's growth during the 1980s.

This central distribution system could not manage volumes of over 10,000 lines to over 280 stores on the very short lead times between store ordering and delivery without major IT support. An ICL mini-computer is installed in each store to support the daily ordering process. Orders are then passed via the data communications network to the central mainframe system, which processes the orders, produces picking and despatch lists for each of warehouses and manages warehouse stocks.

More recently, Sainsbury's has taken the lead in installing scanning checkouts in its supermarkets. These now process over 85 per cent of the sales of almost £5 billion, and are familiar to most shoppers. The laser scanner reads the barcode printed on each packet; this uniquely identifies the product, and reference is then made to a price look-up table in the controlling micro-computer, virtually eliminating all keying of data by the checkout assistant. The process is much faster and more accurate, and also provides a detailed, itemised receipt for the shopper, all of which improve service to the customer significantly.

Alan Jacobs, Sainsbury's Director of Data Processing, reiterates that customer service is a major driving force within the company. But this alone could not justify the huge investment of over £65 million in scanning checkouts. A key initial justification lay in the productivity improvements that scanners generated, both in faster checkout and also in avoiding the time-consuming and costly need to price each packet individually as it was put on the shelf. He also emphasises that, without the fundamental support for IT which exists at the highest levels in the company, it would have been much more difficult to pioneer in this, and many other, applications. Scanning checkouts are a good example of how this faith has paid off. 'We knew that they were a worthwhile investment, but many important benefits have only become really apparent as the installation programme moved ahead. Apart from the direct customer service benefits, they have enabled us to tighten up store ordering and provide an even better match with customers' needs, especially in the fresh produce area.'

Scanning checkouts have also led to new marketing initiatives, such as the 'multibuy', when a shopper gets a special discount for buying, say, four packs of a specific item. The controlling computer automatically recognises when the fourth pack is scanned and applies the discount, without all four having to be scanned together. Because stock in new stores does not have to be priced, the initial shelf filling is much faster, and less staff intensive, contributing to earlier payback on the investment. Alan Jacobs feels that it will be some time yet before Sainsbury's has anywhere near exhausted the benefits from the current scanning technology.

As befits such a successful company, however, Sainsbury's is not resting on its laurels. To improve customer service further by speeding the checkout process, automated payment is being introduced. EFTPOS (Electronic Funds Transfer at Point of Sale) was installed very rapidly, ready for the Christmas peak of 1988 in around forty major stores. Today, in May 1989, over 200 are fitted with this EFTPOS facility. This allows the customer to pay using a Switch debit card, which is read by a card swipe, and checked by the central computer to avoid stolen cards being used. The speed of introduction left major rivals breathless, and the new method has found ready acceptance from customers. It is both faster than cheque payment, and also, as an electronic transaction, substantially reduces the manual procedures and paperwork needed to handle cheques. Customer, retailer and bank all gain.

Alan Jacobs believes that Sainsbury's has established a very strong base in IT support for the business. Major rivals are now tackling similar areas and will eventually catch up, though it will take them some time. The challenge for Sainsbury's is to keep moving smoothly ahead, setting new targets for its rivals.

Pilkington: going for a clear advantage

The Pilkington Group is one of the world's largest producers of glass and related products. Pilkington is also establishing a strong position in the world's opthalmic and electro-optical markets, and is the UK's leading producer of insulation materials. Founded in 1826 as the St Helens Crown Glass Company, Pilkington has grown into an international group with more than 100 subsidiary and related companies in the UK and over 400 other companies in more than thirty countries. The group has a worldwide turnover of £2,572 million, about 77 per cent of which is earned outside the UK.

The St Helens based group headquarters became involved in office automation in the early 1980s, a period which saw huge over-capacity in European glass manufacture, a price war, and a strong pound. The need for productivity improvement to drive down unit costs and maintain margins was paramount. The group has invested heavily in process control and data-processing. There remained a major challenge – improving the performance of their office and administrative systems. In these early days, Pilkington implemented many office automation pilot-systems in their search for a strategic development path for the technology. The early implementations concentrated mainly on the work of secretaries and eventually saw strong gains in work quality, productivity and job satisfaction. The company was very much on a learning curve during this period and its successes and failures were equally important in moving the corporate strategy towards a wide use of IT.

In 1971, Pilkington had a virtual stranglehold on the UK flat glass market with a 71 per cent share. Earlier this decade, its market share collapsed to 52 per cent but has since recovered to 65 per cent. It has become vital for the group to hold steady or increase this UK turnover while it makes the transition from a single product company to a manufacturer of high value-added products with a diverse geographical base.

From 1986 trials with its own glass merchant subsidiary Elders Glass in Gateshead, Pilkington has developed a direct ordering system for its top 100 customers in an attempt to gain competitive advantage. Each has been provided with a PS/2 Model 50 computer, a modem, software and a printer which allow standard order forms to be completed on screen, then hooked up to the Pilkington mainframe via a telephone link to transmit the order. Information about the order is sent back and saved on the customer's computer. A standard order placed with Pilkington is for a 20-ton minimum load that conforms to certain sizes, quantities and types that can be mixed on a lorry. The PS/2 software scrutinises the order and will reject any that fails to adhere to the company's condition of sale. Using the old paper-based system, this function was performed manually by six regional sales offices before the orders were entered onto the central computer. The real significance of the move is as a bid to safeguard UK market share during a time of intense competition from other European manu-facturers.

Dunlop Aviation: taking off with computer-aided engineering

Dunlop Aviation, part of the aerospace division of BTR, started investing in computer-aided engineering (CAE) techniques in 1979. A strategy study, undertaken in 1986, reviewed the existing systems and considered the implications of an integrated approach to CAE. The study examined not only the selection of a new design system but also the organisational environment in which it was to operate. The changes implemented brought together the key design and production engineering functions and permitted closer co-operation through team and project working.

Dunlop Aviation's main customers are aircraft, aerospace and military equipment manufacturers, including Boeing, British Aerospace, Rolls-Royce, Westland, Fokker, McDonnell Douglas, Shorts and Engesa. The company manufactures a range of products that falls into two categories:

- Products related to aircraft wheels and brakes, including associated control systems

- A wide range of other equipment that includes de-icing systems, actuators, engine control systems and power traverse and elevation systems for military vehicles

Many of the company's products include hydraulic and pneumatic control valves and systems and the product range typically includes close-toleranced turned parts, castings, forgings, valves and manifolds with complex drillings and many weight sensitive and stressed components.

The nature of the airline industry imposes strict documentation, procedures and record-keeping requirements on all the company's engineering functions. Dunlop's original investment in CAE was aimed at remaining competitive, having the ability to respond to key customers with short lead times and produce effective products at the right price. If Dunlop adopted a revised organisation structure and an effective approach to integration requirements, the aerospace group could achieve:

- Reduced lead times
- Less handling of information
- Increased use of existing information
- Improved accuracy
- Fewer modifications
- Increase in 'right first time' design
- Increased design analysis
- Fewer test failures and design alterations
- An ability to evaluate more options at an early stage
- Rationalisation, through better use of standard parts
- Increased customer and supplier links
- Improved corporate image

The strategy study, which was triggered by an attempt to cut operating costs, highlighted two interdependent factors that were seen to be crucial to the successful implementation of future CAE systems. These were the choice of an appropriate system with all the required features and capabilities and an operating environment that provided the opportunity to exploit the best and most productive aspects of a true computer-aided engineering approach.

The study also found a number of aspects of the organisation that would need attention:

- A fragmentation and overlap of activities and organisation within engineering, due partly to the way products and departments had evolved over time
- A focus on department rather than projects inhibiting the flow of information
- Difficulties in accessing existing information
- Scope for more rationalisation of parts, methods, tooling and fixtures
- Unwieldy modification procedures causing unnecessary delays
- Shortage of valid cost information
- Limited consideration of a design-for-manufacture approach
- Late involvement of production engineering after design commitments had been made

- Late discovery of the need for changes due to errors or manufacturing problems

- Frequent re-entering, or redocumenting, of existing information

Most significantly, it was concluded that there would be little value in selecting new CAE methods unless there were substantial changes in the organisation and a number of key problems were solved. A CAE approach to the total design and manufacture of a product encourages the blurring of department lines and allows the members of a project team to work simultaneously on a design.

Dunlop established a relatively small CAE group. It was to be concerned specifically with offering a service to the design and production engineering areas and maintaining standards, and procedures. The group also numbered specialists who were viewed as 'functional champions' and who would be charged with implementing specific CAE projects.

A detailed and extensive selection process was initiated for choosing the type of CAE approach that would suit Dunlop and give it the flexibility that it would need in the future. After selection of the system, Dunlop devised a long-range implementation programme that would speed the effective introduction of the CAE system. Dunlop appreciated that proper training was vital if the benefits of the system were to be realised. Awareness training for the initial users began two months before installation. This covered system configuration, an appreciation of CAD and CAE principles, the analysis of a model project and the objectives of the pilot project approach. A flexible training package was formulated with the system supplier and a plan established covering the type and timing of the application courses required.

The pilot projects consisted of three types:

- Recently completed projects that would be copied onto the system and would have a high probability of undergoing modifications or being used in similar designs.

- Analysis-type work, where the accuracy and capability of the system was used to evaluate design problems that could not be handled with manual techniques

- Carefully selected new design work

This work mix was intended to refine the operational aspects of the system and derive early returns from the investment. Some pilots uncovered inaccuracies in dimensioning when copying existing designs onto the system. These errors would have been passed through into manufacturing. The accuracy of the system and the ability to manipulate and evaluate alternative design conditions has helped Dunlop to resolve specific product problems while early savings of £20,000 were achieved by eliminating the need for additional testing. Such progress has helped the system gain acceptance in other departments and paved the way for the first all-CAD project.

IT for the Performing Right Society

The Performing Right Society (PRS) collects royalties for the public use of music of all types, and distributes those royalties to the original authors, composers and publishers of the music. With a turnover approaching £100 million, royalties are collected from radio and television broadcasters, and from business premises of all types where live, recorded or broadcast music is played. The PRS acts as an information company. It receives notifications of about 4 million performances of over 1.5 million works each year and divides the royalties collected between its 25,000 members and the members of similar societies throughout the world.

Its principal business objective was to save at least 100 staff within three years. The PRS felt that the most likely way to achieve this was through increased and more integrated use of IT. Although large parts of the society's activities were already computerised, they were largely discrete systems based on direct replacements of earlier manual systems.

A study was commissioned by a joint management group from both the business and the IT function, who became the project board. The project manager appointed was the senior user manager, who had line management responsibility for over 40 per cent of the PRS staff. He recognised that his responsibilities to the business were only going to be met by regarding IT as the best solution to his problems and he regarded the strategic planning study as too important to delegate. A seven-member team was established, with three middle managers from the core of the business who were joined by an analyst from the IT department to look at the business issues, while a business manager worked with two analysts to study the corporate data architecture. The project lasted three months. The whole team, the project board, and three or four other managers were trained in the appropriate techniques on a two-day seminar. The team began by evaluating the current business strategies, considering the future potential uses of IT, and recommending and justifying a phased implementation plan incorporating both an applications portfolio and a data architecture.

The final report was written by the managers in the team. The report covered both IT proposals directly and a number of non-IT implications. Some of the key benefits of the study included:

- Overcoming existing preconceptions about the applicability of IT to certain operations.

- Overcoming existing differences between senior managers about the objectives, priorities and characteristics of the PRS organisation.

- The ability to see the impact of IT on the organisation as a whole, in a way which is simply not possible when dealing with individual projects. This meant that applications which crossed existing departmental boundaries could be tackled for the first time.

The PRS recognises that a major benefit from their user-led approach has been the commitment shown throughout the organisation. As in all companies there were a number of senior staff who were initially suspicious and doubtful of the potential of IT; the record of delivery of systems was not good, partly because of the reluctance of user-managers to accept their own responsibilities in this area. The strategy study recommended a major re-development of the core systems of the PRS, as well as the corresponding organisation to support the systems. The financial case was approved, and the PRS has now started detailed analysis and design work.

NatWest: banking on technology

NatWest is one of the most successful financial services groups in the world. It is represented in thirty-four countries, has assets of £98 billion and generated profits of £1.4 billion in 1988. NatWest sees its two most important resources as the people it employs and the information it possesses, and regards the key to continued business success as the ability to forge a better relationship between these two resources. IT is seen as the most important catalyst in meeting its objective. That's why over the next five years IT will be the single largest capital investment – some £1.3 billion.

NatWest's overriding principle for this investment will be that it must be business driven, and its business strategy has a strong European focus. NatWest already has footholds in fourteen European countries, including ten in the Community, and wishes to increase its non-sterling income as a percentage of group profits. It views the affluent European theatre as a major target area.

The top business priority will be to defend the UK backyard which generated around £1 billion net profit in 1988. UK competition is already hotting up and undoubtedly Continental predators are already sniffing around but, as overseas banks have found so far, the UK retail financial markets are not easy to penetrate. Secondly, NatWest will be exploiting its existing European operations. It has been developing selected business segments in targeted geographic areas for a number of years (a retail banking presence in Spain, for example).

Finally, NatWest will be looking for new opportunities. Acquisition, joint venture or new greenfield operation all have their place if the opportunity presents itself, and partners will not necessarily be banks. Establishing itself in overseas markets is not new for the company. It did the same in the USA in the mid-1970s and is now the most successful UK bank there.

Because NatWest's business strategies drive its technology spending, the spending concentrates on Europe. The UK dominates but the Continent will become increasingly important. NatWest has established a group technology plan that sets out a technology blueprint which looks five years ahead and is revised annually. It is from this perspective that its needs in terms of technology support for its European business ambitions are assessed. In particular the plan emphasises quality partnership planning with users, group policies in key areas such as standards, procurement, and technical architecture and the need to prioritise projects to reflect business priorities. As the business priority is the UK, the aim will be to continue to expand the UK communications and processing infrastructure and make sure this can be linked to other group systems. Other European technology investments will be relatively small pieces in the jigsaw.

The key is to manage information effectively and ensure users can access what they need quickly and reliably. So NatWest's biggest technology projects are designed to meet these needs. Certainly the single market is a stimulus here. NatWest has a UK customer franchise of 9 million to protect, and the biggest project involves rewriting its central UK accounting system to make it customer rather than account number based. This information systems strategy will allow users to access information faster, increase business volumes without a corresponding rise in staff numbers and enjoy greater opportunities for cross-selling products.

NatWest also has a major telecommunications project to develop its own UK Voice and Data Network. It now has one of the largest networks in Europe, supporting 21,000 visual display terminals. That number is likely to rise to 40,000. The network has been developed to international standards with the long-term vision that the corporation will have an international network into which customers and bank users can plug, irrespective of the make of their equipment. Plans are in hand to expand the network to the USA and, if business needs dictate, links to Continental Europe. The necessary trenches have been dug.

NatWest is a strong supporter of open systems. It does not see a single supplier being able to provide all it needs and sees open systems as a way of protecting its substantial current and future technology investment. Open systems will also give additional flexibility in the face of the fast-moving financial services market place.

Competitive edge means running high quality, reliable systems for its users. With the compound growth of processing and data storage running at 40 per cent per annum, and attention being turned to integrating systems across continents, top notch support is vital. So suppliers to NatWest are being pressed to provide uniform quality support to reflect the global value of NatWest's business.

Telecommunications is seen as a potent weapon for introducing new products and services. Electronic Data Interchange (EDI) is the new shining light and with it comes the opportunity to control costs and accelerate business processes. NatWest plans to remain at the forefront of EDI to help its commercial customers who will be using EDI networks on a European scale and to promote bank services via this medium. NatWest fully supports the United Nations EDIFACT message standard and has dedicated resource working on EDI development (on international trade payments, for example).

As international links become increasingly important, electronic banking will allow delivery of services to a range of customer segments, such as telephone banking for personal customers and cash management systems for large corporates. NatWest already has such systems in place which allow information to be distributed quickly and cost-effectively.

Product development will also be achieved through plastic cards. NatWest now has links with Mastercard and VISA. There are some 50 million cards in the Community and numbers are rising. NatWest is also in the vanguard of both the UK National EFTPOS schemes to be piloted later this year. With its reciprocal links, it now has some 5,800 automated teller machines in the UK and international links are already in place.

NatWest sees its most critical resource as its scarcest – technical skill. It has over 5,000 people supporting technology in Europe and undoubtedly their skills will become more universally accepted, particularly as English is the dominant language of communication. To help recruit, train and retrain these staff, the company has set quality service standards from initial contact with a potential employee. They have dedicated personnel looking after technical staff and have placed great emphasis on offering technical staff structured career paths, competitive remuneration and a challenging environment in which to work. Keeping up the numbers of good quality technical staff is a battle NatWest does not intend to lose.

NatWest sees 1992 as a stimulant to expanding its European operations with priorities being revisited, but no major shifts in its established business strategies. NatWest has set out a high-level technology framework, and is building key projects that can be integrated with European systems when the time is right. Technology will undoubtedly be *one* of the catalysts for business success and this is how NatWest aims to deliver the right products, at the right time, and at the right price.

Glossary

ARPANET Advanced Research Projects Agency Network (US Department of Defense).

artificial intelligence (AI) The capability of a computer to perform functions that are normally attributed to human intelligence, such as learning, adapting, reasoning and self-improvement.

ASCII American Standard Code for Information Interchange.

ATM (automated teller machine) Terminal used by banks and other financial institutions to accept and dispense cash.

batch processing Group of data-processing jobs stored and processed as a unit, typically overnight.

biometrics A security technique which involves measuring some unique feature of a human being and matching it against the stored image.

bit Contraction of binary digit, the smallest unit of information a computer can handle.

blue book A book of standards containing Network Independent File Transfer Protocol set by the JNT.

body part A component part of a message of a specified type, e.g. text or Group 3 facsimile.

browsing The illicit viewing and copying of material contained in a database.

B/TEC Business and Technicians Education Council.

bug Fault in a program.

bus A data highway within a computer.

byte A group of eight bits. An eight bit byte can be used to represent a single alphanumeric character.

card An accessory printed circuit board added to a computer to confer extra abilities and functions, such as high-quality screen graphics.

CBMS   Computer-based message system, a general term for systems providing electronic mail services.

CEN   Comité Européen de Normalisation (European Standardisation Committee).

CENELEC   Comité Européen de Normalisation Electro-technique (European Standardisation Committee for Electrical Products).

computer-aided design (CAD)   Systems used within the design area to generate new designs and modify old ones. Special purpose CAD systems are available for specialised applications such as mechanical assemblies, electronics, architectural, fabric/garment design and plant design. They can also be used in industrial and graphics design.

computer-aided engineering (CAE)   This includes the application of CAD, analysis, and product database systems to improve the complete engineering cycle involved in introducing new products.

computer-aided manufacturing (CAM)   Application of computers to the generation of manufacturing data. This includes data for numerically controlled machines, computer-assisted parts programming, computer-assisted process planning, robotics and programmable logic control. CAM can involve production programming, manufacturing engineering, industrial engineering, facilities engineering and reliability engineering (quality control).

computer crime   As distinct from other white-collar crime, a computer crime involves manipulating a computer system for gain.

computer-integrated manufacturing (CIM)   A highly automated factory in which all manufacturing processes are integrated. CIM enables production planners and schedulers, suppliers, foremen and accountants to share the same data as product designers and engineers.

database   A store of information usually held on magnetic media and accessed by users via a controlling computer.

data encryption standard (DES)   The most widely used algorithm used for secure exchange of information in the commercial world. Devised by IBM, DES is now the subject of an international standard.

data signature   A method of authenticating a document which involves encoding a document or part of a document using the public key encryption system.

debug   To cure the faults in a program.

decision support system (DSS)   A system which provides some of the support needed by an executive to make timely and accurate decisions.

desk-top publishing (DTP)   A system with which complete reports and manuals can be designed and produced. Images and diagrams can be handled alongside text. DTP systems are valuable for technical and user manuals, and can be interfaced to CAD systems for the input of diagrams and drawings.

disaster planning   A branch of computer security dealing with the physical protection of systems against accidents and the provision of back-up systems.

electromagnetic pick-up   A method of eavesdropping on a computer screen which involves picking up its emissions and reproducing them on a second screen.

ESPRIT   European Strategic Programme for Research in Information Technology, funded by the Commission for the European Communities.

expert system   A computer system which contains knowledge concerning a specific problem area. The knowledge can be added during use, so expertise can be extended with experience. They are particularly useful where the rules to solve a problem cannot be exactly defined and where the rules change with time.

extended industry standard architecture (EISA)   Standard PC architecture upgraded to make the best of 32-bit chips.

fibre optic links   The use of thin glass fibre wires to carry digitally encoded material between two points using light as the transmission medium. This is not subject to normal electrical interference and so gives exceptional clarity to the signal, be it voice, text, data or image.

flexible manufacturing systems (FMS)   An arrangement of machines interconnected by a transport system. The transporter carries work to the machines on pallets or other interface units. A central computer controls both machines and transport. It is intended for manufacturing a variety of parts in a random sequence, thus providing flexibility in meeting a fluctuating workload with a wide variety of components.

FLOPS   Floating point operations per second. Normally only applicable to scientific supercomputers.

GOSIP   Government Open Systems Interconnection Profile of which there are two versions, one in the UK produced by CCTA and another in the USA.

hacking   Access to and use of a computer system by a person unauthorised to use the system, who gains entry to the system through by-passing built-in security features.

HZ   Hertz or cycles per second. A measure of the speed of the internal clock which co-ordinates all the activities within a microprocessor.

icon   A graphic representation of a document, task, or activity, displayed on a workstation screen, designed to simplify human-computer interaction. Often used in conjunction with a 'mouse'.

industry standard architecture (ISA)   Conforming to the design of the IBM PC/AT personal computer.

information technology (IT)   A broad approach to the handling of information within a business by applying computing and telecommunications technology.

IPMS   Interpersonal Messaging System, the part of X.400 designed to allow people to exchange messages.

ISO   International Standards Organisation

JANET   Joint Academic Network for the United Kingdom, run by the Network Executive on behalf of the Computer Board for the Universities and the Research Councils.

JNT   Joint Network Team, part of the Computer Board which advises universities and research councils on their use of IT.

Just-In-Time (JIT)   An approach to scheduling which works back from the due date for an order, so that each operation takes place 'just in time' to meet that date. It is a production philosophy which aims at the elimination of all processes which fail to add value.

local area network (LAN)   A low cost, fast and efficient method for connecting personal computers and/or workstations together over a limited area to share data and peripherals such as printers and file servers.

mainframe   A powerful, and in the past, large, computer system which required a controlled physical environment in which to operate. Developments in technology have resulted in considerably smaller devices with similar levels of processing power.

manufacturing automation protocol (MAP) A standard introduced by General Motors for the communication of production information around the shop floor.

mega Million (as in megabyte).

megabyte Memory sizes in computers are measured in bytes, therefore one megabyte computer would have a main memory capacity of eight million bits.

memory See Ram and Rom.

MHE Message handling environment, including users and MHSs.

MHS Message handling system, a collection of user agents, message stores and message transfer agents.

micro One-millionth (as in microsecond).

microchannel architecture (MCA) IBM proprietary design for advanced 32-bit computers which is in contention with EISA as the future standard.

mips Millions of instructions per second. A common but sometimes misleading measure of computer power.

modem Modulator/demodulator. A device which takes the stream of bits transmitted by a computer and converts it into a continuous electrical signal suitable for transmission down a voice grade telephone circuit. A similar device converts the signal to computer language at the other end.

motherboard The main printed circuit board in a computer carrying the central processing unit.

mouse A hand operated control device to support human-computer interaction, and often used for selecting between options on a screen display, and then initiating some action within a computer system.

MS Message Store. A device to store and forward messages on behalf of a user agent on a PC or workstation.

MTA Message Transfer Agent.

multiplexer Device that combines several data streams for transmission down a single data highway.

nano Thousand millionth (as in nanosecond).

NBS National Bureau of Standards (USA), organiser of implementor workshops on various standards, including X.400, and provider of profiles of those standards.

ODA   Office Document Architecture (ISO 8613).

ODIF   Office Document Interchange Format (ISO 8613).

office automation (OA)   The application of computers to automation in offices, including word processing, electronic mail, office diaries, shared spreadsheets, database, and access to external electronic services.

on-line   Continuous connection.

operating system   Complex computer program which marshals the internal operations of the computer itself, allocating space in memory for work files, organising movement of data through the system, etc.

OSI   Open systems interconnection – an emerging set of standards or rules which will enable any computer obeying the rules to be easily connected to any other computer also obeying the rules.

PABX   Private Automatic Branch Exchange. A telephone switching system used on one or more sites of an individual organisation.

password   Unique identifying number that gives its holder access to a computer system.

peer-to-peer communication   Communication between two computers without the need to go through a third computer acting as a supervisor of communications (or host).

piggybacking   A method of gaining illegal access to a system that involves intercepting signals to a terminal and modifying them before passing them to a genuine user.

point of sale (POS)   A term that describes systems used to carry out transactions at the point where sales are made.

program   A self-contained piece of software.

PTO   Public Telecommunications Operator (e.g. Mercury).

PTT   Public Telephone and Telegraph authority (e.g. Deutsche Bundespost).

public key encryption   Encryption technique in which there are two keys – one public, one private. Security of the system relies on keeping the private key secret. The most common type of public key encryption system is called RSA.

quality assurance (QA)   Denotes both quality control and quality engineering.

RAM Random access memory – storage device in which the stored information can be rewritten many times. Ram in the form of semi-conductor memory chips forms the fastest kind of memory in a computer. The size is designated by the number of bits the chip can store. A 256K Ram can store 256 × 1000 bits. A D-Ram (dynamic Ram) is Ram whose memory contents have to be refreshed continuously and therefore use power. An S-Ram (static Ram) is a Ram whose memory contents are retained if the power is switched off.

real-time The computer and user carry on a dialogue, the computer responding immediately to the user's commands and enquiries.

RISC Reduced instruction set computing. Comparatively simple chips that operate at very fast speeds – up to 20 mips and more.

ROM Read only memory – storage device, typically a memory chip or a compact disc, in which the information stored can be retrieved but not altered.

salami technique Type of computer fraud in which a criminal takes a little at a time from a large number of transactions. The classic example is a rounding up and down program for half pennies that has been rigged to round everything up and transfer the difference to a bogus account.

technical office protocol (TOP) A standard introduced by Boeing for the communication of information in the design and production engineering departments.

teletex An improved version of telex, allowing some document formatting and faster transmission.

total quality management (TQM) An approach to business improvement led by the theme of quality. This encompasses everything that occurs in the company, on the premise that this all affects customer satisfaction.

trapdoor An intentional or unintentional weakness in a system that can be exploited by an intruder to gain access to it.

trojan horse The addition to a system of an apparently useful program that contains routines that collect, modify or destroy data.

UA User agent (X.400), a system providing a user with submission and delivery facilities to a message transfer service.

UNIX A computer operating system developed by AT&T, used initially in academic institutions.

user interface   The display systems which a computer presents to an individual, and the associated input devices such as keyboards and pointers.

videotext   A broadcast digital signal or signal across a telephone line or other network which can, when converted, display text material on a television display screen.

voice annotation   A facility to store voice comments relating to a text document, and store the comments with the text so that readers of a document can also listen to the voice comments of those who originated or have already read the text.

voice store and forward   The ability to leave, in digital form, a voice message on a computer system so the message can subsequently be recalled using a standard touchtone telephone handset, and easily relayed to one or many others.

wide area network (WAN)   Methods of linking computers to share data over long distances.

work group computing   A computer system which supports the activities and communications of a number of individuals engaged on some common task or purpose.

X.400   An international standard for electronic mail defined by CCITT, available in two versions (1984 and 1988).

X.500   An international standard for directory services, to enable/ identify users of computer mail services to route messages to users irrespective of their location.

Index